Box Turt

Complete Herp Care

TM

Tess Cook

Box Turtles

Project Team
Editor: Thomas Mazorlig
Indexer: Dianne L. Schneider
Cover Design: Mary Ann Kahn
Design: Patti Escabi

T.F.H. Publications
President/CEO: Glen S. Axelrod
Executive Vice President: Mark E. Johnson
Publisher: Christopher T. Reggio
Production Manager: Kathy Bontz

T.F.H. Publications, Inc.
One TFH Plaza
Third and Union Avenues
Neptune City, NJ 07753

Printed and bound in China,
09 10 11 12 13 3 5 7 9 8 6 4

ISBN 978-0-7938-2895-1

Library of Congress Cataloging-in-Publication Data
Cook, Tess.
Box turtles : a complete guide to Terrapene and Cuora / Tess Cook.
p. cm. — (Complete herp care)
Includes index.
ISBN 978-0-7938-2895-1 (alk. paper)
1. Box turtles as pets. 2. Terrapene. 3. Cuora. I. Title.
SF459.T8C66 2008
639.3'925—dc22

2007048124

This book has been published with the intent to provide accurate and authoritative information in regard to the subject matter within. While every reasonable precaution has been taken in preparation of this book, the author and publisher expressly disclaim responsibility for any errors, omissions, or adverse effects arising from the use or application of the information contained herein. The techniques and suggestions are used at the reader's discretion and are not to be considered a substitute for veterinary care. If you suspect a medical problem consult your veterinarian.

The Leader In Responsible Animal Care For Over 50 Years!®
www.tfh.com

CENTRAL Garden & Pet

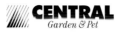

Table of Contents

Introduction

Humans have always been able to observe the slow-moving tortoises and secretive water turtles. These harmless creatures became a part of the spiritual and oral traditions of early mankind, as well as a part of the diet. The turtle is prevalent in the creation myths of the Native Americans, many of whom used their shells for ceremonial purposes. The House of Turtles at Uxmal was built by the early Mayans. It is adorned with numerous life-like box turtle shells carved from stone.

Turtles had a similar effect on the cultures of the East. In Hinduism, one incarnation of Vishnu takes the form of a giant tortoise called Kurma, who saves the gods from demons that were becoming too powerful. The Japanese, Chinese, and other Asian cultures attribute mystical powers of longevity and good fortune to turtles. The tortoise is also portrayed as steady, wise, and noble in many folktales of Africa and Europe. It is no wonder that box turtles continue to fascinate people today.

Overview of This Book

This book is a practical guide to the captive care of both American and Asian box turtle species. These turtles live in a diverse range of natural habitats; housing, diet, and breeding will be discussed for the more common pet species. Box turtles thrive in nature, so we will gather pertinent information about their care from how they live in the wild. Natural history is especially helpful in understanding the housing and dietary needs of box turtles. I will present information in a step-by-step manner that will simplify caring for your box turtle while still promoting its health and overall well-being.

Learning about box turtles may also spur your interest in their long-term survival in the wild. Box turtles in their natural ranges are being affected in many detrimental ways. Collection of Asian turtles for the food and pet markets has decimated whole populations. Human sprawl has fragmented and decreased the habitats of many species of turtles, forcing them ever closer to farms and homes where powered machinery and cars pose deadly hazards. Soil and water pollution have made many areas uninhabitable for reptiles and amphibians. There is some concern that global warming may affect the survivability of hibernating turtles—warmer wintertime temperatures will force them to use up more of their energy reserves. The resource section of this book will direct you to organizations devoted to the education and conservation of

A Turtle or a Tortoise?

Are box turtles the same as tortoises? Europeans often refer to box turtles as "box tortoises." The connotation of the term "tortoise" is that it is terrestrial and seldom enters water except to drink. *Terrapene* and *Cuora* require water to be available at all times—some *Cuora* are aquatic! Technically, all tortoises are classified in the family Testudinidae, whereas *Terrapene* and *Cuora* are from the families Emydidae and Geoemydidae respectively.

box turtles and other turtle species. Books on natural history are listed there as well.

My interest in box turtles began many years ago with the gift of a sickly three-toed box turtle (*Terrapene carolina triunguis*). I named him ET, after the popular movie alien of the time. The name fit, as he was an alien to me. I had never kept a box turtle before, although I had been part of the craze with dime-store red-eared sliders (*Trachemys scripta elegans*) as a child in the 1960s. I remember the horror of finding my beloved tiny turtles unmoving and staring at

The hinged plastron is one of the most defining features of box turtles.

me with lifeless yet accusing eyes. Determined not to let that happen to ET, I began an extensive search for information about box turtles. As I gained knowledge from veterinarians, reptile books, magazines, turtle club newsletters, Internet newsgroups, and other box turtle keepers, my admiration and concern for box turtles grew. My research and experiences in rehabbing, captive management, and breeding of three-toed, ornate (*Terrapene ornata ornata*), and eastern box turtles (*Terrapene carolina carolina*) are the basis for this box turtle care book.

Lastly, I hope this book ignites the excitement and wonder of being a part of the natural world through examining the lives of box turtles. I also hope that these special creatures will have long and fulfilling lives and that their owners will take an active role in conservation efforts.

Acknowledgments

Many long-time keepers and researchers of *Terrapene* and *Cuora* were extremely helpful in providing information and in-depth reviews. I received generous assistance from Sandy and Colin Barnett, James Buskirk, Raymond Ferrell, Heather Kalb, Marty La Prees, Martha Ann Messinger, George Patton, and many others who provided both expertise and photographs for the book. I am indebted to Chris Tabaka, DVM and Sherry Taylor, DVM for providing up-to-date veterinary information and assistance with the health section. Grateful thanks go to Mary Hopson, who provided information on *Cuora* and contributions to the diet section, and to Paula Morris and Pat Osborne for their invaluable help reviewing the manuscript. I am especially grateful to my husband Jeff for his unending support and indispensable advice. Finally, a special thanks to my editor Tom Mazorlig for giving me the opportunity to author this box turtle book as part of the Complete Herp Care series.

Chapter 1

Box Turtle Biology

Our current understanding of modern box turtle species and their long evolution is the result of much research that continues still today. Field observations and DNA research on living turtles and descriptions of fossil remains reveal much about their distribution, paleontology, and genetics. Many scientific papers have been published, and the serious hobbyist will want to read the works of pioneer and current box turtle researchers such as Wilbur W. Milstead, Lucille Stickel, H.A. Allard, John Legler, Charles W. and Elizabeth R. Schwartz, and C. Kenneth Dodd, Jr., to name a few.

The ancestors of modern turtles have been part of the fauna on earth since the Triassic, about 210 million years ago. During this early period of earth's history, land areas were joined into one super-continent called Pangaea. Here the chelonians (the turtles and tortoises, the name coming from their biological order, Chelonia), would evolve in the northern half of this large landmass. Chelonia is one of the oldest living orders of animals; along with their reptilian cousins the crocodiles and the tuatara, chelonians managed to outlive the dinosaurs. Today there are about 290 species of terrestrial and aquatic turtles, tortoises, and sea turtles.

The Species

Understanding your particular turtle's natural history will aid you in providing the best possible care. The following species accounts of box turtles from North America and Asia will give you insights into some of their behaviors and natural habitats. Much more can be learned through further reading, research, and personal experiences.

North American Box Turtles

North American box turtles belong to the family Emydidae. This large family also includes aquatic and semi-aquatic turtles of the Americas, North Africa, and parts of Europe

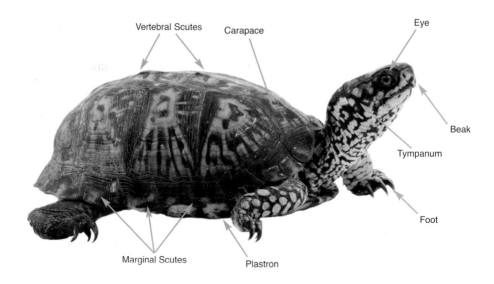

Vertebral Scutes Carapace Eye Beak Tympanum Foot Marginal Scutes Plastron

and Asia. American box turtles are separated from other turtles in this family by the genus classification *Terrapene*. The four species of *Terrapene* are *T. carolina*, *T. ornata*, *T. nelsoni*, and *T. coahuila*. *T. nelsoni* and *T. coahuila* are rarely found in the pet trade.

Terrapene carolina has six subspecies including *T. c. carolina* (common or eastern box turtle), *T. c. triunguis* (three-toed box turtle), *T. c. major* (Gulf Coast box turtle) and *T. c. bauri* (Florida box turtle). Two other subspecies in this group, but rarely seen as pets, are *T. c. mexicana* (Mexican box turtle) and *T. c. yucatana* (Yucatan box turtle). Within *Terrapene ornata* are the subspecies *T. o. ornata* (ornate or western box turtle) and *T. o. luteola* (desert box turtle). The two subspecies of *T. ornata*, along with the eastern, three-toed, Gulf Coast, and Florida box turtles, are the American box turtles most commonly found in the pet trade. Each has a distinctive look, but the ranges of several types overlap, and breeding between the species is not uncommon. Hybrid offspring are especially difficult to identify.

Eastern Box Turtles The four subspecies of the eastern box turtle, *Terrapene carolina*, seen in the pet trade generally inhabit moist deciduous woodlands and other habitats close to trees and water. The forest floor is their home, and it provides them with food, nesting areas, and hibernation sites. All are opportunistic omnivores that feed on items on the ground or otherwise within reach. These items change with the seasons and include earthworms, snails, slugs, small amphibians, carrion, berries, fallen fruit, fungi, plants, rodents, fish, and even the young of ground-dwelling birds. Field studies have shown that some plant seeds have a better germination percentage after passing through a turtle's digestive tract—box turtles therefore may play an important role in seed dispersal within the woodland ecosystem. During hot, dry summers these turtles estivate, or become inactive, by hiding under leaf litter until moist conditions return. During the winter they hibernate (Florida box turtles may remain active all year). All box turtles are diurnal and will retire to a safe place under tree roots, rocks, or low shrubs as evening approaches.

Eastern box turtles dwell on moist forest floors, eating the plants and animals they find there.

T. c. carolina, the common box turtle, is a medium-size turtle reaching lengths of 6 to 7 inches (15.2 to 17.8 cm). It has a high-domed carapace that can be dark brown with yellow, orange, or reddish blotches of various sizes and shapes that form an attractive pattern. There is a prominent mid-dorsal keel. The plastron is all black or can be tan with dark areas. The head and neck of adult males are an attractive mosaic of red, orange, or yellow with additional white and black markings. Scales on the front legs are brightly colored on most specimens. The male's plastron is usually concave to facilitate mating. Males have red irises and the females' are brown. There are four toes on each hind foot and five toes on the front. Eastern box turtles are terrestrial and omnivorous. They can be found from coastal Maine and New Hampshire southward into Georgia and as far west as Michigan, Illinois, Kentucky, and Tennessee.

T. c. triunguis, the three-toed box turtle, is 4 to 6 inches (10.2 to 15.2 cm). It has a high-

Scientific Names

You may have noticed that sometimes there are words in italics that appear in conjunction with the common name of an animal. These italicized words are the animal's scientific name, and each animal should have only one correct scientific name (although there can be a lot of argumentation about the correct name, especially since taxonomic names are subject to change from time to time and from authority to authority). Biologists determine the scientific name of each animal based on what other animal or animals they think it is related to. Most scientific names have two parts. The first part of the name (the generic epithet) tells the name of the genus to which the animal belongs, while the second part (the specific epithet) gives the species part of the name. This combination of genus and species is unique for each animal. Scientific names allow scientists and animal enthusiasts all over the world to talk about each animal without worrying about language barriers or having similar animals being confused with the one they want to discuss.

A scientific name is often abbreviated after the first usage. The genus is abbreviated to the first letter. So, after introducing a species of box turtle as *Terrapene carolina*, it can later be referred to as *T. carolina*. If the author is talking about all the box turtles in this genus, he or she can use *Terrapene* without a species name attached. Some animals have a third name, which indicates that they are a subspecies. Subspecies describe different forms that exist within a species, such as the three-toed box turtle, *Terrapene carolina triunguis,* which can be abbreviated to *T. c. triunguis.*

domed keeled carapace that is often more elongated and narrow than that of the Eastern box turtle. The shell can be olive, brown, or yellowish brown and may have thin lines, dashes, and spots of yellow or brown. The plastron is typically a solid tan, but it may have dark smears around the scute margins. The skin is brown, with orange or yellow scales on the head, neck, and legs. The adult male has red or pinkish eyes and rarely a concave plastron. The females have brown eyes. These turtles often have only three toes on the hind limb, but four toes are not uncommon. They have a large range and are found in western Georgia and westward into Alabama, Louisiana, and northwest Texas and northward into Arkansas, Missouri, and parts of Kansas.

The three-toed box turtle has a high-domed carapace, which can be plain or brightly colored.

T. c. major, the Gulf Coast box turtle, is the largest American box turtle, reaching lengths of 8.5 inches (21.6 cm). The carapace is domed and keeled and widens at the posterior. It is highly variable in coloration; the carapace can be a plain dark olive, dark brown, or black with yellow to orange blotches. The rear marginal scutes of many specimens flare outward, perhaps facilitating their ability to walk through marshy ground. They are also excellent climbers. The plastron is usually unmarked but may have dark splotches. The skin is light or dark brown, and the males have colorful necks and forelegs. The color on the heads of old turtles can fade and turn white. The females have brown irises; the males' irises can be either brown or red. They have three or four toes on their hind limbs. Gulf Coast box turtles are found in the coastal regions of Texas, Louisiana, Alabama, and western Florida.

T. c. bauri, the Florida box turtle, is a small turtle ranging in length from 5 to 5.5 inches (12.7 to 14 cm). Its carapace is elongated, narrow, and high domed and has a mid-dorsal keel. The carapace is dark brown or black with attractive starburst patterns of thin radiating yellow lines on each scute. The plastron is tan with thin lines of brown. Individuals usually have two wide yellow stripes on each side of the head running from the corner of the eyes and down the neck. Males and females both have brown irises. They can have three or four

Gulf Coast box turtles are the largest members of the genus, reaching lengths of 8.5 inches (21.6 cm).

toes on the hind feet. These turtles are found on the Florida peninsula, portions of the Florida Keys, and possibly extreme southeastern Georgia.

T. c. yucatana, the Yucatan box turtle, is medium-sized at 5.5 to 7 inches (14 to 17.8 cm). The carapace is elongated and high-domed; it resembles the shape of the Florida box turtle's carapace. The carapace coloring is variable, but predominately brown or tan, frequently with scattered spots and dark markings that follow the scute margins. There is usually a small hump on the third vertebral scute. The female's skin is brownish, sometimes with dark mottling on the head and light spots on the legs. Adult males have larger heads with white and blue colorations that can extend down the neck. They are terrestrial and inhabit tropical scrub forests in the Mexican states of Campeche, Yucatan, and Quintana Roo on the northern part of the Yucatan Peninsula.

T. c. mexicana, the Mexican box turtle, is a large turtle, reaching lengths of 7.5 inches (19 cm). It looks similar to the Yucatan box turtles, including the small hump on the third vertebral scute. Adult males often have large yellow heads that may contain blue areas, resulting in a striking appearance. The hind foot normally has three toes. Little is known about the natural history of this subspecies. They are terrestrial and can be found in woodland habitats in portions of Tamaulipas, San Luis Potosi, and northern Veracruz, Mexico.

Spotted Box Turtles *Terrapene nelsoni*, which has two subspecies, both of which are called spotted box turtles, is a medium-size turtle, 5.5 to 6 inches (14 to 15.2 cm) long. The carapace, head, and forelimbs bear many yellow spots (especially in females), hence its name. However, this trait is highly variable, and males are often unspotted. Males commonly have larger heads, red rather than brownish eyes, and large bulbous scales on the forelimbs—a trait unique to the species. As in the ornate box turtle, males have a clasping claw on the first hind toe that can rotate forward. Spotted box turtles are restricted to upland portions of the western Mexican states of Sonora, Sinaloa, Chihuahua, Nayarit, and Jalisco. The two subspecies are *T. n. nelsoni* and *T. n. klauberi*. The ecology of both is poorly known, and it remains to be seen whether the two forms warrant subspecies separation.

Coahuilan Box Turtle
Terrapene coahuila, the Coahuilan box turtle, can reach a size of 6 to 7 inches (15.2 to 17.8 cm). The carapace is elongated and dark gray or dark brown in color. Growth annuli may or may not be visible. Males have brown irises, while females' irises are typically light gray. This is the only aquatic American box turtle; it inhabits a small range within the desert-spring ecosystem of Cuatro Ciénegas, Mexico. Loss of habitat due to local agricultural practices may ultimately lead to reduced populations.

Florida box turtles have similar markings to the ornate box turtle, but the yellow stripe behind the eye is distinctive.

Ornate Box Turtles
The two subspecies of *Terrapene ornata* inhabit grasslands, non-agricultural fields, and scrubland deserts. The range of *T. o. ornata,* the nominate subspecies and commonly called the ornate box turtle, may have developed in unison with grazing animals of the North American prairies. The powerful front legs and strong claws of both subspecies are perfect for tearing into manure piles in search of dung beetles, grubs, and flies, and they are proficient in catching grasshoppers and locusts. The desert ornate box turtle (*T. ornata luteola*) has adapted to living in semiarid locations by taking advantage of moist microhabitats found under dense plant cover or in small burrows. During the heat of the day, these turtles retreat to these refuges, where the temperature and humidity remain favorable. Both the ornate box turtle and desert box turtle are omnivorous, with a mostly insectivorous diet, but they will eat carrion, foliage, berries, and cacti (*Opuntia*) pad and fruit.

Yucatan box turtles live only in the northern Yucatan Peninsula and are rarely found in the pet trade.

The Mexican box turtle is a poorly known subspecies found in northeastern Mexico.

T. o. ornata, the ornate box turtle, is a small turtle reaching 4 to 5 inches (10.2 to 12.7 cm) in length. Its carapace is rounder than that of the common box turtle and is flattened on top. There is no raised central keel, although a yellow midline is common. The carapace is dark brown or black, and each scute has 5 to 7 bright yellow lines radiating to form a starburst pattern. The plastron is dark brown with bold yellow lines that form a zebra stripe-like pattern. Skin areas are gray with some darker gray, yellow, or white mottling. Forelimbs have yellow or reddish scales. The female's head is brown with spots of white or yellow. Color dimorphism occurs between the sexes, and mature males obtain a greenish or bluish color on top of the head and have bright red eyes. The first toe on the male's hind leg is thick and flat and can move inward to facilitate grasping of the female during mating. Ornate box turtles occupy a large range and can be found in remnant prairies of Wisconsin, Indiana, Illinois, and the Great Plains states; south to western Louisiana and most of Texas, west to the eastern edge of the Rocky Mountains, and as far north as southern Wyoming.

T. o. luteola, the desert box turtle, looks like the ornate box turtle but is typically more yellowish in overall coloration. There are two different color morphs or phases: a patterned type and an unpatterned type. They are rarely illustrated together, leading to much confusion about the subspecies. The patterned morph has a brown to pale carapace and numerous thin yellow lines on each scute, especially the second pleural scute. Patterns on the plastron often resemble those on ornates, but are more yellowish. The unpatterned type is less common and either straw colored, drab brown, or greenish with little or no trace of striping. The desert ornate box turtle's activity is limited to the summer monsoon months or when humidity is high. Their range includes west Texas, parts of New Mexico and Arizona, and south into Sonora and Chihuahua, Mexico.

Asian Box Turtles

The Asian box turtles belong in the family Geoemydidae; they are sometimes referred to

Little is known about the spotted box turtle. This individual was photographed in Sonora, Mexico.

as Old World pond turtles. This large family includes aquatic and semi-aquatic turtles of Asia, India, Europe, Africa, and South America. The box turtle genera, however, all come from the Asian mainland and nearby islands. There is presently much scientific work being done on these genera. New species, subspecies, and even new genera may emerge from the data. Any discussion of this group's taxonomy could become obsolete in a few years, but the description and care of these turtles will still apply.

The species of turtles commonly called "Asian box turtles" live in widely varied habitats. Only one, *C. amboinensis* (Malayan, Amboina, or Southeast Asian box turtle), lives entirely within the tropics. The others range from the tropics and subtropics to temperate regions. The Malayan box turtle is the most common Asian species in the pet trade. There are several subspecies which are often sold under different names. Another common Asian species is *C. flavomarginata* (Chinese or yellow-margined box turtle), which is now being captive-bred in Europe and the United States. Less frequent pet varieties include *C. galbinifrons* (flowerback or Indochinese box turtle), *C. trifasciata* (Chinese three-striped box turtle), and *C. mouhotii* (keeled box turtle). There are additional *Cuora* species, including *C. aurocapitata, C. mccordi, C. pani, C. serrata, C. yunnanensis,* and *C. zhoui.* Those species are rarely seen in the pet trade and are coveted for zoological collections and breeding. *C. yunnanensis* is now exceedingly rare and possibly extinct.

Researchers have studied the natural history of some of these species since the early 1900s, but there is still much to learn. Field observations have provided diet and habitat prefer-

The Coahuilan box turtle is the only aquatic species of *Terrapene*. It has a small range based around desert springs in the Cuatro Ciénegas Valley of Mexico.

Ring Around the Turtle

Growth annuli are commonly known as growth rings. These are the visible patterns that appear on the exterior of the shell. As the box turtle grows larger, each scute in the shell expands by laying down new keratin. The sum total of these expanding scutes increases the size of the turtle. Unlike the growth rings in trees, the growth rings in turtles do not necessarily correspond to one year. The rings reflect periods of active growth, of which there may be none or even several during any given year.

ences for several species. While all appear to be opportunistic feeders, diets vary from the mostly herbivorous Malayan and keeled box turtles to the highly carnivorous Chinese three-striped to the omnivorous flowerback and yellow-margined. Some are aquatic and others are terrestrial. For this reason it is very important to know your particular species of Asian box turtle and to make sure it has not been misidentified.

Cuora Species C. *amboinensis*, or Malayan box turtle, is a large turtle that grows to 8 to10 inches (20.3 to 25.4 cm). The carapace is domed and keeled and ranges from deep olive to brown. The plastron is highly variable between individuals, from heavy black pigmentation to light tan with just a small dark spot on each scute. The head has three yellow stripes, one that begins above the eyes at the nose and two that begin at the jaw. All three stripes trace back to the neck. The skin on the chin and neck is yellow and the limbs are darker colored. The eyes have slit pupils. Diet is herbivorous, with a preference for aquatic plants. This species is tropical and semi-aquatic, with fully webbed feet; it inhabits ponds, marshes, and rice paddies. Its large range stretches over 1000 miles along the equatorial rainforests from the Nicobar Islands (southeast of India) through Southeast Asia to the Philippines and part of the Malay Archipelago and Sulawesi (formerly known as Celebes Islands). There are four identified subspecies: C. *a. amboinensis*, C. *a. cuoro*, C. *a. kamarona*, and C. *a. lineata*.

C. *trifasciata*, or Chinese three-striped, is a large turtle reaching 8 inches (20.3 cm) in length. The carapace is dark brown and only slightly domed. Three dark stripes run lengthwise on the carapace, one down the middle keel and the other two lines on less distinct keels on the lateral scutes. The plastron is dark brown or black with yellow around the edge. Its other common name, golden coin turtle, derives from the rich yellow or olive green patch found on top of the head. A dark line runs across the side of the face and borders a patch of olive or yellow-orange behind the eyes. The skin is pinkish orange in the inguinal sockets and on the underside of the limbs and tail. They are highly carnivorous and eat insects as well as fish, frogs, snails, and some fallen fruit. These semi-aquatic turtles are found near clear streams in upland areas of Hong Kong, Hainan Island, several southern Chinese provinces, and south into northern Vietnam.

C. flavomarginata, the yellow-margined or Chinese box turtle, is a medium-size turtle, 5 to 8 inches (12.7 to 20.3 cm). The low-domed carapace is elongated and dark brown with a lighter brown center on each scute. A yellow or tan stripe runs down the center of several vertebral scutes. There is often a median keel and sometimes the slight indication of two more keels on the pleural scutes. The carapace scutes have sculptured growth annuli. The plastron is dark brown or black and has a yellow edge all around it—hence the name "yellow-margined." A yellow stripe extends from behind both eyes and down the neck. The skin under the chin and neck is a pale salmon or orange color. The limbs are brownish. Some authors consider this omnivorous species to be primarily terrestri-

The easiest way to tell the two subspecies of *T. ornata* apart is to look at the shell pattern. The ornate box turtle (top) has a few thick yellow lines on each scute, while the desert box turtle (middle) has many thin lines on each scute. There is also a form of the desert box turtle that lacks a pattern entirely (bottom).

al and want to include them in the genus *Cistoclemmys*, but these turtles will enter water and have been found in shallow ponds, upland steams, and steep hillsides under tree and bush canopy. There are three subspecies: *C. f. flavomarginata*, *C. f. evelynae*, and *C. f. sinensis*. They range from subtropical to temperate regions in Taiwan, eastern China, and Japan's Ryukyu Islands.

C. *galbinifrons*, the flowerback or Indochinese box turtle, is a large turtle 7 to 8 inches (17.8 to 20.3 cm) in length. The high-domed carapace has markings consisting of dashes, lines and speckles. The base color of the shell has a pattern of dark and light areas on the vertebral and pleural scutes. A tan line is usually seen along the middle of the carapace. Each shell is a unique and beautiful expression of nature's diversity. The plastron can be mostly tan, or partly tan with dark areas on each scute. The head is light colored in adults and may have spots or streaks of brown or gray with a reddish neck. The skin is brown or dark gray. The three subspecies are *C. g. galbinifrons*, *C. g. picturata* and *C. g. bourreti*. They are omnivorous and one of the most ter-

The Malayan box turtle has an enormous range that includes Southeast Asia, the Philippines, and Sulawesi.

restrial of the species; they are usually found in cool, brushy, mixed woodlands. Their range is limited to the highlands of southern China and northern Vietnam. Some authors want to include this species in the genus *Cistoclemmys*.

C. *mouhotii*, the keeled or Vietnamese box turtle, is 6 to 7 inches (15.2 to 17.8 cm) long. The carapace is high but flattens on top. There is a prominent central keel and two lateral keels. The carapace is tan to shades of dark brown. The plastron is yellow or tan, with or without dark patches on the edge of the

The stripes on the shell and yellowish patch on the head distinguish the Chinese three-striped box turtle from the other species.

scutes. The rear marginal scutes are distinctly serrated—hence another common name, jagged-shell turtle. The skin is brown or gray and often marked with darker irregular fine lines. There may be one or two light spots or black-bordered light stripes on each side of the head. The tail and thighs have pointed tubercles. These terrestrial turtles are usually found hidden under heavy vegetation in forests at moderate elevations. They are primarily herbivorous but relish occasional protein. They are found on the Chinese island of Hainan, parts of southern China, northern Vietnam, Thailand, and Myanmar (formerly Burma) and the northeast Indian state of Assam. This species is believed by some authors to be in the genus *Pyxidea*.

Box Turtle Anatomy

Each box turtle is unique in appearance and personality. The heads and bodies of box turtles vary in size, shape, and coloration, even within the same clutch. With experience, you will be able to recognize the individual characteristics of each turtle. However, all species share the

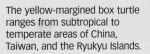

The yellow-margined box turtle ranges from subtropical to temperate areas of China, Taiwan, and the Ryukyu Islands.

The flowerback box turtle lives in the highlands of Vietnam and southern China. It is one of the most terrestrial of the Asian box turtles.

common trait of a hinged plastron, as well as the rest of their basic anatomy.

The Shell

The unique shell of the box turtle is but one of many interesting aspects of its overall anatomy. Inside the hard shell is a soft body with a three-chambered heart. The shell is actually the expanded and fused rib bones that have become overlain by colorful plates of keratin, called scutes. The scutes are what we see, although the bony shell can be exposed as a result of injury or disease. Keratin is the same material that makes up human hair and nails and is a fibrous protein. The turtle's beak, scales, and claws are also made of keratin. The carapace is connected directly to the plastron in the case of box turtles. Other chelonians may have an additional structure called the bridge that connects the top and bottom shells together.

The hatchling's keratin shell keeps pace with the growth of the underlying bones by adding new rings of keratin around the margin of each scute. In this fashion a turtle grows, or "expands" like a balloon. The balance of growth between bones and the keratin scutes is important for normal shell development. Imbalances of growth caused by an improper diet or low humidity can lead to shell deformities.

The Hinge The plastrons of juveniles and adults have a moveable hinge. Strong internal muscles are used to close the plastron against the carapace. The box turtle's hinge is made of tough yet pliable cartilage that develops in the suture between the pectoral and abdominal scutes of the

The keeled box turtle ranges from Hainan and southern China to Assam in northeastern India.

plastron. It is undeveloped in hatchlings and takes several years to form fully.

Circulation and Respiration

The lungs of turtles are large and are located directly under the carapace. Having no diaphragm, other organs in the body are used to push against the lungs to fill and empty them of air. The three-chambered heart has a partial wall called an incomplete septum that helps to keep oxygen-depleted blood from mixing with oxygen-rich blood. It is not as efficient as a four-chambered heart, which keeps the two conditions of blood separate, but it is sufficient for turtles because they do not engage in aerobic activity that demands high oxygen levels. The turtle brain can withstand longer periods of oxygen depletion than the brain of mammals.

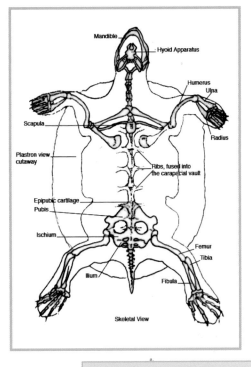

Box turtle skeletal anatomy.

Male and Female Differences

Males and females have many similar features and may be hard to distinguish at first glance. Young box turtles are difficult to sex until their carapace length reaches 3 to 3.5 inches (7.6 to 8.9 cm). Use several sex characteristics to make your determination, as some will be ambiguous.

Adult males of most American species usually have bright red or pink eyes, whereas the females' are brown or a deep ruby color. Adult male ornates will have greenish or faded yellowish heads, whereas the female head will remain dark brown. The plastrons of adult male eastern species have a concave area that facilitates mating. Their hind legs are thick and strong with broad claws, whereas the females have thinner legs and more delicate claws. Males and females also have different tail sizes. The male's is thicker and longer, and the vent (opening for the cloaca) is located well past the edge of the shell. This feature allows the male to place his cloaca next to the female's cloaca during copulation. The females have shorter tails, and the vent is closer to the body.

Age Determination Myth

Counting growth rings (annuli) on a box turtle shell is not a reliable method for determining a turtle's age. The rings actually represent changes in growth rates—not the passing of time. Young turtle shells may grow as many as several rings in a single year. Some pet turtles have consistent eating patterns throughout the year and may not always add a new ring. Wild box turtles typically stop growing new visible rings after about 18 to 20 years. The annuli are actually narrow indentations in the shell and will wear down with age.

The Senses

Box turtles have highly developed senses of sight and smell. They are particularly attracted to the colors red and yellow—not surprising when you consider that most turtles' heads and necks have red or yellow spots and they probably see these colors quite well. Box turtles rely on their sense of smell when eating and can have feeding problems when it is impaired. Turtles will put their nose close to food and take a sniff, probably checking to see whether they approve of the meal. If they have nasal discharge that interferes with smelling, it is almost impossible to entice them to eat.

Turtles hear tones in the 100 Hz to 700 Hz range and hear many sounds that a human can hear, except high and very low frequencies. However, they are likely able to sense low vibrations with their feet or shell, as an approaching human rarely arrives unnoticed. Thus people seldom observe active behaviors in turtles. By the time we notice them they have stopped walking, foraging, or whatever else they do with their time! Box turtles lack ear openings, but they have a specialized scale, called the tympanic scale, on each side of the head. The scale protects the middle and inner ear canals. Infections in the middle ear can cause the tympanic scale to swell outward from the accumulation of caseous pus.

Locomotion

Box turtles have a typical reptilian gait in which one foreleg moves in close tandem with the opposing hind leg. A turtle with a missing limb cannot adjust its walking style, but usually is able to manage with the defect. The plastron can become thin in the area under the missing limb as a result of abrasion. A box turtle's foot can have three, four, or five toes. Some, like the three toed, Florida, and Mexican box turtles have three, or sometimes four toes on the hind limbs and five on the front limbs. Other box turtles normally have four on the hind foot and five on the front. Box turtle have strong claws and use their forelegs to burrow into the ground to hibernate. The females use their hind limbs to dig their nests.

Semi-aquatic box turtles have webbed toes. Most box turtle species can swim, and some seem to really enjoy it. However, the terrestrial box turtles tire easily and sometimes drown when they cannot find easy egress from deep ponds or pools.

Box turtles are very good climbers and have been known to climb up chain link fences, short brick walls, and shrubbery to the dismay of their owners. Many pets have been lost because of their ability to climb. Adult box turtles are quite fast as well. Although their walk appears leisurely, an eastern box turtle can sprint and increase its speed by 72 percent if provoked. Ornate box turtles are about three times faster!

Aging in Box Turtles

It takes ten years or more for box turtles to become adults, and they can live for many more decades. One keeper had a three-toed for over 50 years; there are other anecdotal accounts of box turtles living for a hundred years or more! Although their brain is not large, box turtles learn and appear to retain memories. They remember the best places to hibernate, to lay eggs, and to find fruiting trees and vines. Research has shown they do not suffer from age-related infirmities and do not appear to become feeble.

Ectothermy

The most important attribute of box turtles for the pet owner to consider is that they are ectothermic, or cold-blooded. They cannot heat their bodies through metabolism. Box turtles regulate their internal temperature behaviorally by exposing their body to warm or cool sources. If they are cold and need to warm up they will bask in sunlight or under a heat lamp. They will hide under shade or in burrows or soak in water to cool down.

This characteristic makes caring for turtles more complicated than caring for a dog or cat. The owner must provide housing with a temperature gradient that will allow the turtle to thermoregulate and function properly on all levels: from locomotion to maintaining sufficient heart rate and efficient organ performance. We'll discuss how to create a temperature gradient in the housing chapter.

Acquiring a Box Turtle

Many of us consider box turtles to be fascinating creatures, but we may not fully understand their needs as pets. Box turtles, like most other reptiles, are high-maintenance pets and do not offer the cuddly attraction of the family cat or dog. Due to their longevity and dependence on the pet keeper, one should think long and hard before deciding on acquiring a box turtle. However, there are many owners like me who get great satisfaction from having box turtles! This chapter will present the various considerations and methods for obtaining a box turtle and describe the signs to look for in getting a healthy one.

Wild Collection

Not long ago, people had the option of going to the woods and picking up a North American box turtle. A summer rite for many children was to find a turtle and take it home to observe for a few months. Most turtles managed to survive on the lettuce and the occasional worm and were often released when school started. But as more of the turtle's range became smaller due to urbanization, deforestation, and over-collection, their numbers started dwindling. Only a few states still allow native box turtles to be taken out of the wild. Even if your state still allows it, please do not collect wild box turtles! They should be left in their native habitats in order to breed and multiply. Egg and hatchling mortality rates are very high—the removal of even a few box turtles can doom the population in a given area.

Many states also regulate the possession of box turtles. For example, my state requires permits for all varieties of American box turtles, and they have to be implanted with Passive Integrated Transponder (PIT) tags. Know your state laws and comply with the regulations. Federal laws prohibit the sale and transportation of turtles smaller than 4 inches (10.2 cm). For this reason, very young turtles are not sold in pet stores.

Until a few years ago, many thousands of American box turtles were taken from the wild

Most states regulate or prohibit taking box turtles (eastern box shown here) from the wild.

Five Ways You Can Protect Wild Turtles

Even if we cannot personally help turtles in the wild, we can avoid being part of the problem. Please follow these five suggestions to help protect wild box turtles.

1. Do not buy pet store turtles that appear to be wild-caught; big, breeding-age box turtles usually fall into the wild-caught category.
2. Do not take turtles out of the wild.
3. Do not disturb the nests of turtles.
4. Educate your family and friends about the plight of turtles.
5. Support organizations that protect turtles and their habitat.

If safe to do so, always help a box turtle trying to cross a road. Notice the direction it is heading and take it to that side, well away from the road. Do not move the turtle to what you consider a safer place. American box turtles have a homing instinct and will try to return to familiar grounds if removed from their home range.

and sold to dealers for the European and Asian pet trade. Many died during shipment and others later died from stress-related diseases or improper husbandry. That shameful practice has been stopped thanks to the efforts of conservationists and hobbyists. An international agreement regulating trade in wild animals and plants has been useful in curbing the commerce of many endangered species, including box turtles. It is called the Convention on International Trade in Endangered Species of Wild Fauna and Flora, or CITES. The United States is a partner in this agreement and added American box turtles to the CITES II list in 1996. Because of this agreement, box turtles can no longer be shipped into or out of the United States without special permits. All Asian box turtle species are also covered under CITES. Because of these state and federal regulations, few options remain for collecting or purchasing box turtles.

How to Obtain a Box Turtle

Pet stores in some states are still permitted to deal in box turtles, but you should be cautious about how they were obtained. Large, breeding-age adults are almost always wild-caught. Because this adds to the depletion of natural populations, ask the pet store to provide its customers with only captive-bred box turtles. Although often more expensive,

Injured Turtles

If you find an injured turtle, veterinary care will be the best option. Transport the injured turtle (in a small box or bucket lined with a thick towel) to a wildlife rehabilitator as soon as possible. Many cities have wildlife care centers. Your state's department of wildlife should have a listing of licensed wildlife rehabilitators, or you can contact the nature centers at local state parks for advice on how to find one. Your veterinarian, local herp society, or humane society may also know of someone who can help.

captive-bred animals are usually better adapted as pets and are generally healthier.

Existing turtle owners often must give up their pets and sometimes will place them up for adoption. Call humane societies in your state and ask to be put on a contact list for potential box turtle adoption. Another option is to join herpetological or turtle clubs, which often have specimens needing homes. These clubs are also great places to get first-hand information on caring for turtles. Most do a good job of educating owners and helping with local conservation of turtles. Private breeders of box turtles are listed in herpetological magazines and on the Internet.

The Healthy Box Turtle

Although American box turtles are more common, the Asian species are just as personable and make great pets for anyone willing to provide proper housing and diet. The checklist below is suitable for all species of box turtles and can be used to help you determine the condition of the turtle. When adopting, you may not have the option of choosing your new box turtle. I wholeheartedly recommend adopting sick or damaged turtles if you are willing and able to give treatment. Sickly box turtles can often be treated with simple TLC, but some may need expert veterinary care. Make sure you understand what you are getting into beforehand and use the checklist below as a guide.

1. Hold the turtle in one hand. It should feel solid and heavy as you gauge its size. It should not feel light, or hollow like an empty box. Anorexic turtles will need immediate veterinary care. Severe dehydration will cause the turtle to be lightweight as well.

2. Look at the carapace. Check for unhealed cracks or flaking scutes. Neither the American nor Asian varieties shed their scutes. Normal wear and healed injuries may be present, but beware of any active shell damage. The shell should be symmetrical, with no lumps

or soft areas that might indicate signs of nutritional deficiencies or infections.

3. The head should be symmetrical, with no lumps on the sides of the head. Head lumps might indicate an abscess of the middle ear or a cyst. An open or incomplete tympanic scale suggests a previous infection.

4. The eyes should be open and clear, not sunken in or dull. Discharge from the eyes, inflamed nictitating membranes, or eyes sealed shut could mean a respiratory infection, severe dehydration, or vitamin A deficiency. Look for mites around the eyelids. The lids may be swollen, and you will see tiny parasites around the eyes under slight magnification.

House Before Turtle

It is important to create suitable housing before actually getting your turtle. You will need time to monitor and adjust the temperatures of the enclosure. This also means your turtle doesn't have to sit around in a dark, cold box while you scramble to assemble the enclosure.

5. The nostrils should be open, not crusty or plugged. Signs of discharge could indicate a respiratory infection.

6. Look into the mouth. You can apply gentle downward pressure on the lower jaw with the end of an eraser to get the mouth to open. The tongue should be pink—in some ornates it will be blue. The mouth should have no discharge or signs of mouth rot—cheesy yellow blotches or red spots on the tongue or palate. Sick turtles will often breathe with an open mouth. The beak should not be cracked or overgrown.

7. Pull on the legs. The turtle should pull away from the pressure. The legs should not be swollen. The toes should be well formed and without overgrown claws. Cracked, dry skin may be a sign the turtle was kept in overly dry conditions.

8. Check the skin on the neck and in the leg sockets (inguinal pockets). Skin should be smooth and pliable, not dry, puffy, and red, as this may indicate possible edema or subcutaneous bleeding. Look for cuts, lumps, ticks, and dryness.

9. Look at the tail. Fighting, desiccation, or predator attacks may cause loss of the tail. The vent should be clean, with no swelling, discharge, or odor.

10. The plastron should be without cracks or cuts and the hinge undamaged. Shell rot often occurs on the plastron. Look for peeling scutes, bad odor, or redness under the plastron, which might indicate septicemia.

The above checklist should not be used to diagnose problems. All newly acquired box turtles should be seen by a veterinarian who is familiar with box turtles. Turtles under stress can succumb to opportunistic pathogens when their immunity is low. Accidents do happen in which they become injured (e.g., dog bites). When a veterinarian is needed, you do not want to waste time trying to locate one. A working relationship with a veterinarian is an important element in providing good health care for your turtle. There is more information on turtle vets in the health care chapter.

A healthy box turtle's eyes will be open and bright with no swelling or discharge.

Acclimation

New turtles should be taken to a reptile veterinarian for a thorough checkup. If you have other turtles, the turtle should have a quarantine period, regardless of the checkup results. A bacterial or viral infection in a new turtle may go undetected for months and later spread to other turtles with dire consequences. Use a quarantine period of three to six months for American box turtles, and 12 months for Asian turtles (they are more prone to bacterial and parasitic diseases). Although this may seem lengthy, the safety of your turtles depends on your efforts!

If the animal remains healthy during the quarantine period, it is ready to be placed into its regular enclosure. If you have species of turtles from different continents, they should be housed separately on a permanent basis. If this is your only turtle, the acclimation period may be as short as a few days. Afterwards, closely observe the turtle in its new home, looking for clues to its habits so that you can provide care as needed.

Quarantine Terrarium for Terrestrial Box Turtles

A quarantine terrarium can be made from a very large plastic tote measuring 24 in. x 18 in. x 16 in. (61 cm x 46 cm x 41 cm) or 18 gallons (68 liters). A large glass aquarium can also be used if you cover the sides with paper so the turtle cannot see out. One end of the enclosure should be filled with a

Caution

Box turtles (and most other reptiles and most birds) can be carriers of the bacterium *Salmonella* and therefore should not be pets for very young children or individuals with compromised immunities.

thick layer of moist sphagnum and peat moss; the other side should contain a shallow dish of fresh water big enough for the turtle to sit in. Place a waterproof hide box on the moss side and flat pieces of shale or tile pavers on the side in which the water dish will be placed.

A heat lamp with a 50 or 75 watt incandescent light bulb should shine on the water and shale for 12 hours a day. Maintain a temperature of 80° to 85° F (27° to 29° C) on that side. Use a good digital thermometer to check the temperatures at turtle level. You may need to adjust the

Newly acquired Asian box turtles (flowerback box turtle shown here) should be kept in quarantine away from other turtles for 12 months.

bulb wattage or height to achieve the correct conditions. A double fluorescent light fixture providing both UVB and UVA light should be placed across the moss side and the temperature maintained around 75° F (24° C) for American box turtles and 80° F (27° C) for Asian species. Keep the terrarium in a quiet area of the house and make sure no drafts blow into the container. A nighttime drop in temperature is natural for the turtles, and no additional heat is needed if the temperature stays above 65° F (18° C). However, tropical Asian species should be kept at nighttime temperatures above 75° F (24° C).

Aquatic Asian species can be quarantined in aquariums like those described in the housing chapter. Never mix American box turtles with Asian box turtles. A pathogen that is tolerated by one type of turtle may cause a serious illness in the other! Likewise, it is best to not house different species of turtles together.

Quarantine Care

Over the next few weeks soak the turtle daily in a shallow pan of tepid water, deep enough to reach halfway up the turtle's sides. Soak for 15 to 30 minutes each time. Feedings should follow the recommendations in the diet chapter. Let the turtle rest between observations and handling.

Remove and examine any feces. The droppings should be dark and well formed and not contain worms or undigested food. During long quarantine periods, the bedding should be replaced weekly at first and regularly thereafter so that contamination is totally removed. An obvious cost in time and money is involved with long-term quarantines, but the efforts may save your collection from potentially fatal diseases.

Housing Box Turtles

Proper housing for box turtles is as important as a wholesome and complete diet. Improper housing can stress a turtle, affect its appetite, and lower its immunity to disease. In this section, you will learn how to provide housing that is safe and appropriate. Outdoor enclosures generally provide the best environments, but adequate housing can be made indoors as well.

Field studies of box turtles in their natural settings give us many clues to understanding their needs in captivity. In the wild, their home ranges can be from half an acre (0.2 hectares) up to many times that size, depending on the available resources. However, captive box turtles do not require such a large living space as long as we provide all the essential features of their wild habitat.

Box turtles are ectothermic (cold-blooded) and cannot generate body heat from within themselves like mammals or birds. However, box turtles have a remarkable ability to control their body temperature by behavioral mechanisms: moving in and out of the sun, burying themselves in moist cool substrate, and spending time soaking in water. At optimal body temperatures, box turtles can perform all the necessary actions in life, such as walking, foraging, mating, egg formation, and digestion of food. A well-planned outdoor or indoor enclosure will provide the necessary warm and cool regions, shelter, and proper access to water.

Even terrestrial box turtles, such as Eastern box turtles, will enter the water to cool off on hot days.

Species Considerations

North American and Asian box turtles obviously are from different continents, but more importantly, they are from different climate zones. Eastern box turtles are generally found in moist woodlands, marshes and meadows in temperate climate zones. However, two *Terrapene carolina* subspecies, *T. c. mexicana* and *T. c. yucatana*, are found in tropical deciduous scrub forests and are rarely available in the pet trade. The Coahuilan box turtle is a protected aquatic species unavailable to the pet trade and is found in the desert-spring ecosystem of Cuatro Ciénegas, Mexico. The rare spotted box turtle is found in a narrow strip of tropical deciduous forests in the Pacific coastal foothills of western Mexico. The husbandry of these four rare turtles is not discussed in detail, although their care would be similar to that of their northern relatives.

Ornate box turtles are found in prairies and scrublands of the Great Plains states, which are typically dry and hot in the summer months. The desert ornate subspecies is found in the desert scrublands of the American Southwest. Although the climatic conditions would appear to be quite different from those of the eastern box turtle, both species live in similar microhabitats. Ornate and desert ornate box turtles find cooler and more humid environments within underground burrows or under dense shrubs.

Chapter 3 Glossary

ectothermic: Having a body temperature that varies according to external environmental temperatures.

friable: Soil that is easy to dig into

habitat: Natural environment of an animal; also refers to housing that reflects naturalistic conditions

thermoregulation: Control of body temperature; turtles and other reptiles do this by moving to warmer or cooler places as needed.

The various box turtles from Asia inhabit different climatic zones—housing requirements will depend on the particular species. The two aquatic members are the Malayan and Chinese three-striped. They inhabit warm ponds and streams within forests. The yellow-margined box turtle is found on land (but near water) under the dense tropical forest canopy. Flowerback and keeled turtles are found in temperate terrestrial habitats. The various Asian species should never live in mixed groups or be housed together with American box turtles.

Outdoor vs. Indoor Housing

Box turtles should live outside whenever possible. Even if only during warm summer months, or a few hours each day, box turtles should be given time outside to receive the benefit of sunshine, fresh air, exercise, and some honest turtle foraging. If you live in the natural range of box turtles, it is easy to create suitable permanent outdoor housing. Indoor enclosures can be created using artificial lighting and heating; if done correctly they will provide adequate housing for most turtles.

Some pet owners may want to allow their box turtles to roam freely in a room within the home. This is not a safe option for the turtle or the pet owner. Box turtles can carry and

Preferred Optimal Temperature Zone

The preferred optimal temperatures zone (POTZ) is the temperature range in which a reptile is best able to digest food, grow, reproduce, and heal. The POTZ for box turtles varies depending on the particular species's geographic distribution. When on medication, turtles should be housed at the high end of their POTZ to insure proper drug uptake by the body. A nighttime temperature drop of 5-10°F (2.8-5.5°C) is advisable and mimics nature.

spread bacteria of the genus *Salmonella*, which cause a well-known and potentially dangerous contagion in humans. Turtles may become lost in the house and suffer deteriorating health without food and water. In addition, typical household temperatures, drafts, and low humidity are not suitable conditions for box turtles.

Box Turtle Age and Size

Enclosures for hatchlings have different considerations from those for juveniles or adult turtles. Hatchling enclosures are discussed in detail in the breeding chapter. In short, hatchlings must be housed indoors to protect them from harsh weather conditions and from predators such as large birds, raccoons, dogs, ants, and rodents.

Multiple Turtles

If you have more than one box turtle, there are several factors to consider when deciding on cohabitation. Adult females and immature turtles of similar size and mild temperament can usually be housed together. Males are often aggressive toward each other and may require separate housing. They can also be very persistent when attempting to breed. The mounted animal (male or female) is easily stressed and may become injured. The males of aquatic Asian species are especially aggressive and can inflict serious injuries to females. Mature males should be housed with mature females for only a brief period during breeding—just long enough to complete courtship and mating.

Box turtles may become stressed in close proximity to others and should be able to distance themselves from pen mates. Hygiene problems can develop in overcrowded enclosures as feces and urine accumulate, creating a breeding ground for bacteria. I recommend housing one or two adult females, or a single male, in an indoor enclosure with at least twelve square feet (1.1 square meters) of space. Outdoor pens should be made as large as possible and include plantings, logs, caves, and mounds that serve as visual barriers between the turtles. Finally, American and Asian box turtles should never be housed together. Not only are their specific needs different, but one type may lack immunity to pathogens carried by the other.

Sick or Injured Turtles

Sick or injured box turtles should not be housed outside or with other box turtles. A turtle with respiratory illness, open wounds, puffy eyes, or diarrhea should be kept in a warm indoor hospital tank (see the chapter dealing with health considerations) to protect it from flies and allow for close monitoring.

Outdoor Enclosures

Appropriate outdoor housing is an enclosure that provides the turtle with near-natural conditions and adequate space. Make sure the local climate is suitable for your particular turtle. Some eastern box turtle and ornate box turtle subspecies can be housed in the same type of enclosure (they live in similar microhabitats in the wild). Many Asian species can be housed outside as well. However, their outdoor exposure should be limited to those times of the year when daytime temperatures are above 80° F (27° C) and the nighttime temperature does not drop below 65° F (18° C). You can accommodate the need for warmer temperatures by modifying a greenhouse for the turtles' use whenever temperatures are cooler. During cold months, they should be housed indoors where ideal temperatures of 80° to 90° F (27° to 32° C) can be maintained.

My current turtle pen is a free-form enclosure divided into two main sections to separate the males from the females as required by state regulations. I used a number of different materials to create a pen that is both functional and attractive. Aluminum flashing is buried to a depth of 10 inches (25 cm) under the perimeter walls to prevent the turtles from digging out. The wooden or rock walls are 16 to 20 inches (41 to 51 cm) tall and are capped in places that might allow a turtle to climb out. The total pen size is about 400

Too Many Males Spoil the Peace

A male to female ratio of 1:4 is best when housing turtles together in outside pens. This will divide the male's attention away from any one female, which would cause that female great stress. A large pen with abundant cover and hide boxes will also aid females in escaping unwanted attention.

square feet (37 square meters) and is large enough to house as many as 20 turtles—more than I ever plan on having!

Location

Before constructing the enclosure you must first choose a location. Pick an area that gets good sunlight throughout the day, preferably away from the sides of your home. You can always create shade with plantings and low structures. This variation in sunlight will allow the turtles to thermoregulate their body temperatures. Be aware of any potential for flooding in the area you choose. If you plan to breed or overwinter box turtles within the pen, it is critical that it receives good sunlight and has good drainage.

Outdoor Substrate

After choosing a location, determine whether soil enhancements are needed to create a moist, friable substrate. Some native soils become dry or hard-packed during the summer. Box turtles need a moisture-retaining substrate into which

The author's outdoor box turtle pen. A three-toed box turtle is soaking in the rocky pool.

they can dig to escape hot weather. Hard-packed soil is often slick after rains, making it difficult for an overturned turtle to right itself. Depending on the soil, you many need to add leaf mulch, grass, peat moss, sand, and chemical-free topsoil to create a soft, loamy substrate.

Escape-Proof Pens

Over the years, I have experimented with turtle pen designs and have seen numerous pictures of pens from other turtle owners. All types of materials have been used for building the walls: chain link fence, wood boards and posts, vinyl or aluminum sheets, concrete blocks, bricks, rocks, and stucco walls. Choose a material that you can work with and will safely house your box turtles.

The walls need to be high enough to prevent escapes. Walls 16 to 20 inches (41 to 51 cm) high are usually adequate. This height will prevent a turtle from climbing on another's back

Special Considerations for Female Turtles

Females need places to nest, especially if they are part of a breeding colony. They prefer sunny locations with soft, moist, well-draining substrate at least 8 inches (20 cm) deep. Even if you are not breeding them, a female turtle can lay fertile eggs up to four years after mating and infertile eggs throughout her life. Without the ability to nest, a female turtle might retain her eggs and develop life-threatening complications from dystocia, or egg binding. So, even if you have no plans on breeding your female box turtle, you should provide a nesting site in her enclosure.

and pulling itself over the top. The walls need to be sturdy enough so that wind gusts, other pets, or people cannot knock them down. Since most turtles are good climbers, you may need to make corner barriers and add inward-projecting ledges on top of non-slippery walls. If you use chain link fencing, cover the bottom portion with something the turtle cannot see through. This will stop the turtle from pacing at the wall and will also prevent it from climbing up the fence.

My early pen designs were simple rectangles made of vinyl sheets cut to fit a frame made of PVC piping. I was living then in southeast Texas, so wood was a bad choice because of termites and rotting. The vinyl sheets were connected to the frame with screws. Vertical PVC pipe legs extended 10 inches (25 cm) downward from the corners of the frame and were sunk into the ground for rigidity and anchoring. I buried a row of bricks next to the wall just below the surface to discourage the turtles from digging at the walls. This also supplied

You can make an outdoor box turtle pen out of vinyl sheets and PVC pipes.

the turtles with a hard surface to walk on and helped keep their claws trimmed. Half-size cinder blocks or other strong material can be buried 12 inches (30.5 cm) under each wall to prevent tunneling escapes. The 16-inch (41 cm) tall vinyl walls were too slippery for the turtles to climb up. For rougher surfaces like brick or wood, be sure to cap the corners. Alternatively, you can build a screened lid for the enclosure to prevent escapes.

Watering and Feeding Stations

Large shallow reservoirs of fresh water should be provided for drinking and soaking. Plastic plant saucers and heavy plastic roller paint pans (previously unused) work well. Recess them in the ground to offer easy access for the turtles. The dishes should be placed in shade to prevent overheating.

Designate eating areas near overhanging plants so that shy turtles will feel safe. Create a substrate for the eating area using flat rocks or brick pavers. Placing food on a hard surface will make clean-up easier. When the turtle strikes at food such as live worms, the hard surface will help trim any beak overgrowth. Each turtle should have its own eating area so that you can monitor the types and quantity of food being consumed. This also helps to keep aggressive turtles from bothering others during feeding.

Moisture

During dry periods, the pen should be watered to maintain humidity, cooler temperatures, and moist, friable soil. Adding an automatic sprinkler system to the pen is a great investment in drought-prone areas. Adverse climatic conditions such as dry, hot weather can contribute to dry skin, swollen eyes, middle ear abscess, and upper respiratory infection. Cold, damp weather can reduce a box turtle's immunity as well. Do your best to provide ideal conditions even when turtles are housed outside.

Naturalistic Features

Foraging, exploration, and exercise are part of box turtle behavior and are beneficial to overall health. Adding items to the enclosure will help evoke these natural behaviors. Occasionally add a new item to stimulate the turtle's curiosity. Avoid placing anything close to the walls that might aid in escape attempts. Berry bushes or dwarf varieties of fruiting trees can be planted if the pen is large enough. You can also grow edible vegetation inside the pen such as ever-bearing strawberries, nasturtiums, red clover, and leaf lettuce. Wild mushrooms, mosses, and weeds growing in the enclosure can be sources of food for the turtles or for the insects they enjoy eating. Planting groundcovers and adding leaf litter piles will provide areas for hiding and for the creation of "forms." Forms are depressions turtles make in the substrate near rocks or logs or among plants. They allow the turtles to breathe the humid air of the moist substrate, which contributes to the turtle's well-being. I use blue fescue or other bunching grasses, low-growing shrubs, and pachysandra because they are hardy and can withstand having turtles digging at their roots. Growing plants can aid these escape artists, so keep them cut back from walls and corners.

Predator Proof

Penned turtles must be protected from predatory animals, including pet dogs. Many animals are harmful to box turtles such as raccoons, coyotes, foxes, opossums, skunks, large birds, snakes, and rodents. I have to protect my turtles at night and during hibernation. Since my outdoor pen is too large to cover, I must place the turtles into a smaller nighttime enclosure that is covered and latched. This outdoor "safe" pen is similar to the vinyl pen

Flat rocks make good feeding stations in outdoor pens. The rock will help wear down the beak. This is an ornate box turtle feeding on a mealworm.

described earlier, but is built with a sturdy wooden frame and heavy aluminum sides. A hinged cover is made like a screen door, using wood framing and strong wire mesh. The nighttime pen has plenty of room and cover for the turtles in order to minimize the stress of daily moves. The safety factor far outweighs the inconvenience to turtle and human!

If you live in the suburbs or city, there may be other considerations for the safety of your turtles. Keepers have had their pets stolen, intentionally or unintentionally released, even poisoned by toxic runoff. Think of everything that can go wrong with the pen and then find the solution before your turtle gets hurt.

Maintenance of Outdoor Pens

Cleaning and maintaining your outdoor pen is a never-ending job. Water bowls need to be rinsed out daily and refilled with fresh water. Water bowls should be thoroughly cleaned once a week with a solution of biodegradable dish soap and weak bleach solution (1 teaspoon of bleach per gallon, or 1 ml per 1.3 l), then rinsed well and dried. Leftover food and any observable feces should be removed daily. The sun's ultraviolet rays help to kill bacteria, and rain will dilute some accumulation of feces and parasites, but you can expedite the process. During summer months, occasionally add leaf mulch and turn the soil over. This will help minimize the turtle's contact with feces or urine and disrupt the concentration of parasites.

Insect Problems

Although box turtles eat some insects and arachnids, certain ones may be harmful to the turtle. Chiggers, mites, ticks, and even mosquitoes are known to prey upon box turtles. Fire ants are especially dangerous (they can kill box turtles) and should be eradicated as soon as discovered. Smaller ant mounds can be destroyed by dousing with copious amounts of boiling water. Large mounds are often too extensive for this method. Use a commercial fire ant product for the larger infestations. Follow the manufacturer's directions and use the product as far from the turtle pen as possible. If the fire ant mound is within the pen, remove the turtles before treating. Put the ant poison in small containers and poke large holes on the top and sides. The ants will crawl into the containers and take the food to their mounds. Do not sprinkle poison directly on the ground within the turtle enclosure. Remove the containers before rain to prevent ground contamination. Return the turtles to the pen only after the fire ants have been eliminated.

Mites are usually a problem only if the turtles are housed close to snakes or lizards. When turtles are kept outdoors, this pest may be present but rarely become a problem. With bad infestations, mites can be seen moving around the eyes, the nares, or the cloaca. Mites feed on blood from the soft tissues in these areas and can cause lethargy, anemia, and other complications. Infected turtles should be placed in an indoor hospital tank and treated accordingly (see chapter on health care). Once the turtles have been removed, clean the enclosure and turn over the soil. If indoor enclosures are affected, throw away all the bedding and clean everything else with soapy hot water and strong bleach solution at a dilution of one half cup per gallon (118 ml per 1.3 l). Rinse well and dry.

Mosquitoes and chiggers are often found around turtles. By keeping turtle pens moist, we inadvertently provide the perfect environment for mosquitoes and chiggers. Because they can carry diseases harmful to both humans and turtles, mosquitoes should be eliminated if present in large numbers. Aerate ponds and stock with fish that eat insect larvae. Keep turtle water dishes filled with fresh water and remove sources of stagnant water; cleaning the water dish daily will prevent mosquito larvae from maturing into mosquitoes. Apply insect repellent containing DEET to exposed skin and clothes to protect yourself.

These nighttime pens have screened tops to prevent predators from attacking the turtles.

Indoor Habitats

Box turtles are very active and benefit from having room to exercise and explore. If confined to a small space, they suffer from what can best be described as depression. They lose their appetite and claw at the walls, or sit lifeless in a corner of the enclosure. One of the joys of keeping box turtles is observing their range of behaviors, something best achieved in a roomy, well-enriched habitat. Some aquarium makers are now designing tanks especially for reptiles. These aquariums have more floor space and shorter walls. Some are even divided for use with aquatic turtles. However, most are only suitable as temporary housing for quarantined or sick turtles.

For permanent housing of terrestrial turtles use large pre-made pond forms, bookcases, or kiddie pools. Aquatic box turtles can be housed in large aquariums, plastic horse troughs, or commercially available water turtle tubs. After you have added the substrate soil or water, hide logs, and other tank furnishings, these containers will be heavy. Placing the set-up on a table or platform with rollers will allow you to move it outside for easy cleaning. Whatever you use for the indoor habitat, make sure that it will be easy to clean.

Clean the water features in your outdoor turtle pen frequently to prevent mosquitoes from breeding.

Custom Terrestrial Indoor Housing

The best indoor housings are custom designed and should be made as spacious as possible. Most keepers will go through several sizes of enclosures before realizing turtles are more entertaining when they have plenty of room. The following description of an indoor enclosure for terrestrial turtles was made by Sandy Barnett of the Mid-Atlantic Turtle & Tortoise Society. She uses a sturdy bookcase laid flat on its back and with the shelves removed. Reinforce the back of the case with extra screws. The case is at least 12 inches (30 cm) deep, with 12 to 13 square feet (1.1 to 1.2 square meters) of floor space. A moisture-proof liner of heavy-duty plastic (>6 mm) or pond liner is added, or the interior surface can be coated with a waterproof but non-toxic finish. The corners of the liner are neatly tucked so any water will not get trapped. The draped edges of the liner are stapled (use a staple gun for best results) along the rim, and the entire edge is trimmed with a strip of wood that overhangs the inside edge, both to further secure the liner and to prevent turtle escapes.

Substrate

Turtles live on dirt and leaves in their natural environment, but these become messy in an indoor setup and may contain parasites, molds, or bacteria. Suitable bedding must be able to retain moisture. Sphagnum moss can hold up to 20 times its dry weight in water. I like to use a mixture of sphagnum moss and milled coconut husk fiber (sometimes called coir) or peat moss. The combination retains moisture, is cheap and easy to replace for cleaning, and turtles seem to love it. If you use milled coconut, soak the brick in a large bucket full of warm water and it will expand to many times its original volume. Rinse it several times to remove the dust. Rinse the sphagnum moss and mix it with an equal amount of coconut husk. Other commercial beddings that can be used are finely shredded hardwood mulch, cypress mulch, top soil, potting soil without perlite or addititives, and terrarium moss. Experiment with your own mixture and use one that suits the turtle. Put about 5 to 6 inches (13 to15 cm) of bedding into the bookcase enclosure. Place flat rocks or tile pavers on top of the substrate in several places to create feeding and basking areas.

Reptile carpet does not retain moisture and will not satisfy your turtle's desire to dig and hide under the surface. Never use pine bark or cedar shavings, since the aromatic oils can cause permanent damage to the nasal lining and even death to reptiles. Other commercial beddings to avoid are walnut shell chips, recycled newspaper bedding, rabbit pellets, cat litter, and aspen shavings. Gravel and pure silica or calcium sand are not recommended, as they can cause impactions in the digestive tract.

Humidity

Humidity is an important factor in box turtles' growth. Research has shown that dry conditions contribute to deformities of the shell. Use a hygrometer (available at many pet stores) and maintain the humidity between 70 and 90 percent. Spray the bedding as often as necessary and place water dishes under lights to increase the humidity. If your home is dry, you can place Plexiglas or a similar rigid plastic sheeting over part of the habitat to retain moisture as long as good ventilation is maintained. You can also use a warm-air room humidifier.

Water

As with outdoor enclosures, a water feature must be provided to allow for drinking and soaking. A "pool" can be made from a large plastic plant saucer or plastic paint roller pan, or from a modified photograph developing tray. Hatchlings can overturn in deep water and could drown. They should have access to very shallow water only—one-half inch (1.3 cm) deep or less. You can soak them in deeper water if you supervise carefully. Make sure the water dish is recessed into the bedding for easy access. Rinse it out daily or whenever soiled, and scrub clean with hot soapy water and bleach once each week. Rinse well to remove any bleach residue.

Perlite

Do not use potting soil that contains perlite. These are small white particles of puffed volcanic glass used in some commercial potting soils. Box turtles often have an urge to eat small white pebbles in their quest for calcium, but perlite is indigestible and may cause intestinal blockage.

Heating

Indoor enclosures require lighting and heating that will mimic natural outdoor conditions. Provide both a warm and cool side so the turtles can thermoregulate their body temperature. Place a digital thermometer in both areas and monitor temperatures being generated at turtle level. It is important not to guess the temperature. As the seasons change, recheck the temperatures and adjust the wattage and height of the bulbs to maintain the proper ranges. Care must be taken to keep any kind of heat source away from the turtles or bedding. All lamps get very hot and must be used with caution. Help prevent fires by using sturdy lamp supports, careful wiring, and use of arc-fault interrupt breakers.

Hardwood mulch is one of several acceptable substrates for indoor box turtles. A keeled box turtle is shown here.

The number of lamps and wattage of the bulbs will depend on the size of the space you are trying to heat. Incandescent bulbs, heat lamps, ceramic heat emitters, and infrared lights can be used as heat sources. For large spaces, mercury vapor lights can be used with special caution. These lights produce heat as well as ultraviolet light, but they are very bright and get hot and are not suitable for small indoor enclosures or where people spend a lot of time. Ordinary incandescent bulbs are the safest to use in such cases.

Adjust the wattage and position of the heat sources to achieve a temperature of 80° F (27° C) on the warm side and 70° F (21° C) on the cool side for American box turtles. Add a basking area at 85° F (29° C). Flowerback and yellow-margined turtles can be housed at these temperatures as well. A drop of 10° F (5.6° C) at night is acceptable for most box turtles. The Chinese three-striped and Malayan box turtles will need a warm haul-out area of 90° F (32° C) and water temperature of 82° F (78° C). If it gets cooler than 80° F (27° C) at night for these two species, use a low-wattage infrared light to keep the enclosure warm.

Lighting

Box turtles are diurnal creatures; they are active in the day and sleep at night. They require both light and dark cycles. Two types of ultraviolet light are important to a box turtle's health, but both are invisible to human eyes. Ultraviolet A and B (UVA and UVB) light sources provide the spectrum of light beneficial for good health. The best way for your turtle to get UV light is by allowing it to spend time outside. Even indoor turtles can be placed in daytime pens for a few hours for exercise and sunlight. UVA light stimulates the turtle's appetite by making the color of food appear more natural. It is the same wavelength plants use to grow and may benefit the turtle in other ways not yet understood.

UVB light is necessary for the metabolism of calcium, an essential process especially for turtles. Vitamin D3 (cholecalciferol) is synthesized by cells within the skin when it is exposed to UVB. This vitamin is used in the transformation of calcium into a form the body can use. Sunlight's UVB rays are blocked by glass panes or screens. If the turtle cannot be placed outside each day for a short period of time, you must provide artificial sunlight. UVA light tubes are made by several companies as plant lights. Several pet supply manufacturers make UVB light tubes specifically for reptiles. All UVB light tubes gradually lose their efficiency and should be replaced every three months for growing young turtles and every six to nine months for adults. Mercury vapor bulbs do not need to be changed as frequently but should be replaced every 12 to 18 months. A support structure for UVB fluorescent light fixtures can be made for the bookcase enclosure by using several pieces of pre-finished shelf lumber. Construct the support so that the UV lights hang about 16 to 18 inches (41 to 46 cm) above the turtles. Attach a two-bulb shop light fixture so both UVA and UVB bulbs can be used. Add a basking light via a clamp-on fixture, or attach it to a stable free-standing light stand. Connect the lights and heat lamp to a timer to provide consistent lighting—12 hours of light and 12 hours of darkness.

A complete indoor box turtle habitat includes ultraviolet lights, heat lamps, hiding places, and a soaking area.

Indoor Furnishings

Thoughtful furnishing of the indoor habitat is important for limiting boredom and stress. Hollowed-out logs, broken clay pots, and plants will provide cover and can be used as hides. Make sure items from the outdoors do not contain nuisance insects. Real or fake plants should not have any sharp points that could injure the turtle. Do not arrange objects in a manner that could trap or crush a turtle, such as an unstable rock formation. Small turtles can become wedged between furnishings and even die from heat exposure if stuck near a heat lamp.

Maintenance of Indoor Habitats

Indoor enclosures must be cleaned on a regular basis. Without the benefit of sun and rain, bacteria and parasites can accumulate to dangerous levels if enclosures are seldom cleaned. Pick up all uneaten food within one hour after feeding. Feces should be removed from bedding whenever detected. Rinse and refill water dishes with clean water if feces are observed following soakings. Water dishes should be cleaned weekly with a dilute mixture of bleach and water. Replace the bedding monthly, especially if the habitat is small. A regular maintenance schedule can spare you the trouble of dealing with parasites and many illnesses.

Sanitize the cage and furnishing with a dilute solution of chlorhexidine (4-6 tablespoons per gallon water). If a strong bleach solution (1/2 cup per gallon of water) (118 ml per 1.3 l) is used to sanitize, be sure to rinse and dry well after cleaning. Chlorhexidine is safe for reptiles, but residual bleach left in the cage can cause health problems. A large enclosure should be cleaned once a month unless there are several turtles living in it. Small tanks or crowded conditions will lead to concentration of germs in the habitat and should be cleaned more often.

Indoor Housing for Asian Box Turtles

During the cooler seasons or in those areas where Asian box turtles cannot be kept outside, indoor housing must be used. Depending on the species, some can be housed in terrestrial setups like the one described above. However, others require an aquatic habitat. Be sure you know your specific Asian species. The Malayan and Chinese three-striped are tropical aquatic turtles and will need a large water feature and overall warmer temperatures.

Heat From Above

Many reptiles bask on warm rocks to soak up "belly heat"; box turtles, however, prefer a direct overhead heat source. Hot rocks, heating pads, and heat tapes are preset at the factory to a temperature that can cause tissue and shell damage and should not be used with box turtles.

Yellow-margined, flowerback, and keeled box turtles are terrestrial and can be housed in enclosures similar to American species, provided the temperature ranges are increased to mimic their subtropical norms.

Aquatic Tank Housing

For the aquatic species, create a habitat that is warm, has lots of clean water to swim in, and has a haul-out platform for basking. A 50-gallon (190-liter) aquarium is a good size for a single turtle. Fill the tank with 8 inches (20 cm) of water and heat to 82° F (28° C) using an aquarium water heater. Surround the heater with a wire screen to prevent the turtle from damaging it.

Add a small platform that lies just above the water surface. The platform can be a shallow plastic tray filled with flat pebbles that rests on several bricks placed in the

A custom-built enclosure for Malayan box turtles. Filtering the water makes maintenance much easier.

bottom of the tank. Using an elevated platform allows for more swimming room and provides a hiding area underneath for times when the turtle feels threatened. Some keepers support the platform with acrylic bars that have been attached to the sides of the tank with waterproof epoxy. If you have a gravid female, a deeper tray should be used—one that is at least 5 inches (13 cm) deep. Fill it with sandy soil instead of pebbles so that the female may use it to dig a nest. Place a heat lamp directly over one side of the platform to provide a basking area at 90° F (32° C).

Aquatic turtles eat and defecate in the same water. A large-capacity external filter will help keep the water clean but will not replace the need for periodic water changes. Decorative items are not necessary in the tank, but a pile of flat rocks can be pleasing for the owner and will give the turtle another place to haul out onto. Aquatic plants can be added that will provide both food and cover for the turtle. Covering the back and sides of the tank with decorative paper will give the tank visual appeal and can make the turtle feel more secure.

Custom Aquatic Enclosure

When housing multiple aquatic box turtles together, consider the custom enclosure designed by box turtle keeper Mary Hopson. These turtles can be aggressive and will likely require more space than typically available in aquariums. Males are especially aggressive and should be housed separately from females, except for short unions if breeding is desired.

Build a wooden box on a sturdy platform (with optional rollers) measuring 72 in. x 48 in. x 20 in. (183 cm x 122 cm x 51 cm). Line the box with thick plastic or coat the interior with a non-toxic waterproof finish. A large water feature is made by draping a rubber liner over another wooden box measuring 48 in. x 42 in. x 10 in. (122 cm x 107 cm x 25 cm). Line the bottom of the "pond" with gravel or flat rocks to create a water depth of 8 inches (20 cm). An aquarium heater and large-capacity external water filter must be used to keep the water warm and clean.

Create a small land area immediately adjacent to the pond by adding 2 inches (5 cm) of charcoal, 6 inches (15 cm) of sandy top soil and then top with 2 inches (5 cm) of cypress mulch and sphagnum moss. The level of the dirt should now be about level to the water feature. Use light poles or construct an overhead wooden structure to hold the UVA and UVB lights and heat lamp 16 to 18 inches (41 to 46 cm) above the turtles. Heat the basking area to 90° F (32° C), but allow for a cool area that is lower by 10° F (5.6° C). Cover a portion of the enclosure with Plexiglas to maintain a high humidity in the range of 70 to 90 percent. The pond can be cleaned as you would an aquarium and the land area refreshed as needed.

Diet for Box Turtles

Proper nutrition is one of the cornerstones to good health for your box turtle. Along with suitable housing, it will ensure that your turtle remains healthy and happy for many years. Many of us can recall younger days when we fed iceberg lettuce or hamburger to a box turtle that had wandered into the neighborhood. These foods are not necessarily bad, but when used exclusively over long periods of time they can lead to life-threatening diseases and terrible deformities. The key to avoiding these problems is a varied and nutritious diet consisting of foods from five groups: animal matter (proteins, fats, etc.), fungi, greens (leaves), fruits, and vegetables. The following section presents the basics of box turtle nutrition, how to select the menu, and some tips on how to prevent problems with picky eaters.

Chapter 4 Glossary

carrion: Dead animals

cuttlebone: Hard internal structure of the cuttlefish which is a good calcium source for turtles

fauna: Animal life

flora: Plant life

forbs: Plants with a non-woody stem such as wildflowers and weeds

The Omnivores

The American box turtles are omnivores, consuming both animal and plant material in relatively equal amounts. The yellow-margined and flowerback box turtles have omnivorous diets similar to that of the American species. However, the Malayan and keeled box turtles are primarily herbivorous, whereas the Chinese three-striped box turtle eats a mostly carnivorous diet; diets for these turtles are discussed later in this chapter.

Research into box turtle eating habits is limited, but stomach content analyses of American box turtles show a remarkable diversity of fauna and flora in their diet. Field observations show these box turtles to be opportunistic feeders. They consume animal matter such as beetles, insect larvae, gastropods, flies, spiders, isopods, other invertebrates, carrion, and just about anything else they can catch or find on the ground. They also eat available seasonal fungi and plants including berries, fruits, seeds, forbs, mosses, and roots. Box turtle pets should be given a similar wide variety of foods in order to meet nutritional needs and to mimic their seasonal eating preferences.

In deciding on a meal plan for your omnivorous turtle, almost any fresh food imaginable will have a place in the diet. There are a few items, such as spinach and cabbage, that are often listed as bad foods for turtles. Spinach is high in oxalic acid, a chemical that binds calcium so it cannot be used by the body. Turtles are especially

The American box turtles are omnivores. This is an eastern box turtle enjoying a meal of blueberries, greens, turtle chow, and other items.

susceptible to calcium deficiencies because of their bodies' high demand for the mineral. Cabbage, broccoli, and other brassicas are often listed as bad foods because they contain goitrogens, which interfere with the uptake of iodine. Eaten in excess and in the absence of other foods, these types of vegetables could lead to calcium deficiencies or to a goiter or kidney problems. But both are excellent sources of fiber, vitamins (e.g., beta-carotene, B-complex, C, E, and K) calcium, potassium, trace minerals, and micro-nutrients. They can actually be good food for box turtles if fed in moderation and supplemented with calcium or cuttlebone. The real danger lies in feeding any one food item exclusively to your box turtle.

Animal-Matter Foods

Invertebrates make up a large part of the contents found in wild box turtle stomachs. Keepers can find many of these foods in pesticide-free backyards and gardens; earthworms, white grubs (C-shaped beetle larvae found underground), grasshoppers, cicadas, June beetles, pill bugs, millipedes, butterfly larvae, snails, and slugs. Some turtle owners grow their own earthworms or mealworms. Most of us will likely need to purchase other foods to meet the diversity and quantity requirements.

With the ever-increasing popularity of exotic pets, commercial insect farms are now breeding and raising crickets, mealworms, wax worms (bee moth larvae), superworms (*Zoophobas*), blood worms, nightcrawlers, and silkworms, all of which can be purchased year-round. Some can be gut-loaded before feeding to your turtle. In addition, manufacturers of pet foods are producing dried and canned insects that can be used when live insects are scarce. Great strides have been made in formulating healthy and palatable dry foods specifically for box turtles.

Certain meats that are intended for human consumption can also be a part of the captive turtle diet. Lean ground sirloin or skinless poultry that is prepared in a healthy way (by boiling or microwaving) can be fed to turtles as a part of a varied diet. However, these muscle meats are low in calcium content and should be lightly sprinkled with calcium prior to feeding. Low-fat dog food or cat food (canned or dried) can be used on occasion if given

Gut-loading Insects

Crickets and mealworms can be gut-loaded two days before use. Do this by feeding the insects a high-calcium invertebrate food. Many commercial products can be found on the Internet. You can also use sweet potato, a high-quality tropical fish flake, or dry cat food. To provide the insects with moisture and added nutrients, use leafy greens, such as turnip or dandelion greens.

in moderation and as part of a varied diet. Box turtles should not eat other processed foods like hot dogs and deli cuts, high-fat items, or dairy products.

Plant-Matter Foods

Wild box turtles live in a veritable Garden of Eden, where all the plants needed to thrive are available for the taking. Vegetation makes up a large part of the wild turtle diet, and its importance cannot be over-stressed for pets. Stomach contents of wild box turtles include fungi, berries, forbs, leaves, mosses, buds, roots, and fallen fruits. Gathering pesticide-free wild plants for your turtle can be a fun activity if you have access to meadows, wooded areas, or even

Ornate box turtles are adept at catching katydids and grasshoppers. These insects often form a large part of a wild box turtle's diet.

vacant lots. Keepers often gather wildflowers, young leaves of weeds (e.g., dandelions and clover), edible mushrooms, mulberries, elderberries, blackberries, persimmons, and sea grapes—depending on your location, of course. If your turtles are outside, allow the native grasses, mosses, and edible plants to grow freely within their enclosure.

Vegetables and fruits purchased from the store should be fresh rather than canned. Frozen vegetables can be used in a pinch and are convenient when your turtles must be cared for by a pet sitter. Many grocery stores carry spineless cactus pads and fruit (*Opuntia*), as well as greens such as chicory, mustard, and watercress. Aquatic plants are important for Malayan box turtles and can be purchased from tropical fish shops or suppliers on the Internet. Turtles have a limited capacity to intake food, so I keep an eye on nutrition by focusing on certain parts of the plant. For example, I use the rinds of summer squash rather than the less nutritious pulp. Knowing the nutritional content of food can be very instrumental in caring for underweight or sick turtles, as they need to consume more calories and nutrition with each bite.

Most vegetables are safe for turtles. Hard vegetables should be grated and steamed. Carrots only need to be grated, whereas winter squash and sweet potatoes can be grated and then lightly steamed or microwaved. Corn, spineless prickly pear (make sure to remove any tiny sharp spines), and green beans can be served raw or cooked. Vegetables that contain goitrogens are cabbage, broccoli, Brussels sprouts, and cauliflower. They can be used if given in moderation and as part of a varied diet. Ripe fruits include cherries, apples, peaches, strawberries, blackberries, grapes, tomatoes, kiwi, cantaloupe, mangos, papayas, and most others.

Leafy greens are another important part of your turtle's diet. Red leaf, romaine, and bibb lettuces, kale, dandelion, and field greens are a few that can be used. Even the much-maligned iceberg lettuce has a place in the box turtle diet. I give it to my outdoor turtles as an occasional treat on hot days—the high water content of the lettuce is much appreciated. Spinach and kale contain oxalic acid but can be used in moderation as part of a varied diet if calcium is supplemented. Poisonous plant substances, such as rhubarb leaves, potato leaves, and tobacco leaves, should never be part of the diet. Avocados may or may not be poisonous to turtles—they are toxic to birds—but it is better to be safe than sorry; avoid feeding them to your turtle.

Fungi make up a large part of the diet of wild box turtles. The turtles' moist woodland habitats usually have an abundant supply of mushrooms—each new season bringing forth new varieties of fungi within reach of hungry box turtles. Box turtles have been known to eat poisonous mushrooms with no ill effect. To be safe, use only edible kinds.

I actively look for morels (*Morchella deliciosa*) in the spring and feed the turtles any that are wormy. I also use shaggy ink caps (*Coprinus comatus*), fried-chicken mushroom (*Lyophyllum aggregatum*), field mushrooms (*Psalliota campestris*), and *Russula* mushrooms (e.g., *Russula lepida*). Local food markets often have chanterelles, oyster, and shitake mushrooms. Some box turtles will relish mushrooms, while others may not show much interest. Always try to include fungi in the diet, as they are a source of valuable nutrients.

Turtle Chow

Commercial turtle chows are now available and can be used occasionally as part of your turtle's diet. The first ingredients listed should be proteins. Don't use a turtle chow that is made mostly of grains. Turtle chow already contains vitamins and minerals, so the only supplement needed is calcium, which should be sprinkled or scraped onto the food. Hydrate the dry food slightly and mix with fruits, greens, and vegetables for a palatable meal.

Meal Plan for Omnivores

Wild omnivorous box turtles consume plant and animal matter in roughly equal proportions. This relative ratio of food sources is the basis for the omnivore meal plan. At each feeding I offer a blend of items from the five food groups: animal matter, vegetables, greens, fruits, and fungi. I change the selections from each group with every meal in order to provide variety in the diet. By consistently offering food in this way, your omnivorous turtle will eat healthier. A chart in this chapter lists many of the healthy choices from the five groups. You can also add foods that are available in your location. If you live in Hawaii, add passion fruit! Florida residents might include wood roaches. Eliminate guesswork by adding one food item from each group, but remember to vary the ingredients each time to mimic the turtle's natural feeding patterns.

Preparing the Meal

Select one of the vegetables (20 percent of the meal) and chop it into small pieces, cooking lightly if needed. Prepare the remaining 30 percent non-animal portion by combining equal volumes of fruit, fungi, and greens; chop as needed and mix together. You now have half of the meal prepared.

Box turtles relish all types of grubs. You can find them under turf and sod and beneath rotting logs.

Choose one of the animal-matter options and add 50 percent by weight to the vegetarian portion. After mixing everything together, divide and give 2 to 3 tablespoons (30 to 45 ml) to each adult, or about 1 tablespoon (15 ml) for young turtles. You can add whole berries on top for visual and olfactory appeal. Apply a light sprinkling of calcium and vitamin supplements to the meal once each week (see section on supplements later in chapter). Very young turtles can be given similar foods as for adults, but the meal should consist of 75 percent animal matter, and vegetables should be finely chopped. After one year, switch to a diet that is closer to 50 percent animal

eater. Excessive protein in the diet causes shell deformities, kidney damage, and early death. These box turtles should be given a variety of the plant-based foods described earlier. Malayan and keeled box turtles relish aquatic plants and dark greens.

Feeding Frequency

Factors such as age, health condition, and the time of year should determine how often to feed captive turtles. Hatchlings and young turtles can be fed every other day. Healthy adult turtles can generally be fed every third day (more often if they are underweight). Overfeeding can lead to certain dietary problems. When excess food is available, some turtles may begin to selectively eat only favorite foods, and actually lose nutrition in the process. On the other hand, ravenous eaters may develop excessive weight gain. After several months of preparing meals, you'll begin to learn the appropriate amount of food for your turtle. Adjust portion sizes so that only a small amount of food remains after the turtle finishes eating.

Each turtle should have a separate feeding dish or flat rock so that its individual eating behaviors can be observed. Sick turtles will often go "off their feed" and shy turtles may not eat when pen mates are close by. Some turtles may eat only when fed under a plant or in a hollow log. Handicapped turtles may need special attention such as hand-feeding. Blind turtles can be taught to eat by the sound of a clicker or, if placed into a small tub containing plenty of food, can usually find their meal by smell.

Supplements

It is also important to provide calcium separate from meals so the turtles can self-regulate intake of this vital mineral. A cuttlebone placed in the pen provides both calcium

Feeding Schedule Based on Age and Health Condition

Young box turtles can grow too fast and adult turtles can become obese if they are fed too often. Set up a regular feeding schedule for your turtle depending on its age and health condition.

Feeding Frequency	1 to 2 days	2 to 3 days	3 to 4 days	4 days
Age	Hatchlings up to 1 year old	1 to 3 years old	3 years old to mature adult	
Health Condition	Underweight	Recovering from illness		Overweight

and trace iodine, and it will help the turtle keep its beak well trimmed.

In addition to the cuttlebone, you should add a calcium supplement and reptile vitamins to food once a week. Use a calcium supplement that contains no added phosphorus but does include vitamin D3, especially for turtles housed indoors. Vitamin D3 is important for the metabolism of calcium and is naturally formed by cells in the turtle's skin when exposed to UVB light. Avoid giving excessive amounts of vitamin D3, because of possible overdosing.

Water

One of the more common ailments found in pet turtles is dehydration resulting from a lack of available fresh water. Without it, the body is unable to process food or eliminate the toxic by-products of metabolism. Water should be available at all times in large shallow dishes that the turtle can easily climb in and out of. Since turtles may also use the water dish as a place to eliminate body wastes, the water should be changed everyday or as often as necessary to keep it clean.

Feeding Issues

Two feeding problems are often seen in box turtles: food fixation and inappetence. Both of these problems can be prevented or remedied with some know-how and persistence on the part of the keeper.

Vitamin A Deficiency

A deficiency of vitamin A often results from an improper diet, especially one low in plant-based foods. Symptoms may include dry, peeling skin, accumulation of caseous pus in the eyes, and swollen nictitating membranes. However, these symptoms may be the result of other conditions, such as dehydration.

Vitamin A supplementation should never be given without a thorough review of the diet history. It is possible to overdose vitamin A when added as a supplement or given by injection. A better choice is to alter the diet by increasing the plant matter. Vitamin A is naturally obtained from beta-carotene in dark green leaves, yellow or orange vegetables, and some fruits. It is also found in some fish and the organ meats of mammals. An occasional drop of cod liver oil onto food can also be helpful.

Cuttlebone provides box turtles with calcium and keeps their beak trimmed.

Food Fixation

Turtles can become fixated on a single food, for example, mealworms. When this happens, they often "train" their keeper to always give them their favorite item.

To get around this stubborn behavior, gradually wean them onto different foods. For example, if your turtle is fixated on mealworms, try the following: mix 12 to 16 mealworms together with 1/4 cup (60 ml) of finely chopped sweet potatoes (cooked or baby food variety), chopped romaine, and chopped strawberries. The turtle will probably pick through the plant matter and eat only the mealworms, or may even turn his nose up to the whole meal and walk away. In this case, do not back down by offering just mealworms the following day. Instead, prepare the next meal with the same proportions. Continue this until the turtle begins to eat, and gradually replace the percentage of mealworms with more of the other foods. Avoid the problem of food fixations by changing the meal choices at each feeding.

Inappetence

Box turtles stop eating for various reasons. There are a few things you can do to help stimulate their appetites. Check that the temperature and humidity are still in the optimum range. Raise the temperature a few degrees to see if eating resumes. You can also try misting the turtle just before feeding—wild turtles are often stimulated to eat after a rain storm. Offer a new food, or perhaps a pinkie mouse. If the turtle is housed outside, hot or dry weather might cause it to stop eating. Try watering the enclosure. The approach of autumn will also decrease the turtle's appetite. If there are no environmental reasons for the lack of appetite, take the turtle to a veterinarian to rule out any health issues if eating does not resume after a few weeks. Although turtles can survive months without eating during hibernation, they cannot remain healthy for long if the hunger strike occurs while they are active.

Chapter 5

Box Turtle Health Care

Box turtles can be hardy pets and will rarely become sick if kept in suitable housing and fed a complete diet. Stress from substandard husbandry practices, however, can suppress the immune system of captive reptiles. When this happens, opportunistic bacteria, viruses, fungi, and parasites can more easily attack the turtle. Of equal importance to treating a sick box turtle is the discovery and elimination of the underlying causes. This chapter will help you recognize the signs of illness, when and how you yourself can treat them, and when to seek a veterinarian's expertise. You will also learn proper husbandry practices to avoid the onset and recurrence of many of these illnesses.

Inexperienced turtle owners may have difficulty distinguishing between normal behaviors and those that might signal a developing or ongoing illness. In the wild, weakened turtles are easy pickings for a predator and have adapted by attempting to mask signs of debility. A good understanding of normal behaviors will help you to know when something is wrong. Observation is the real secret to keeping box turtles healthy. Pay special attention to your turtle while it feeds, basks, soaks, walks, swims, and interacts with its surroundings. Changes in these behaviors may signal illness. Internet resources can connect you with veteran turtle owners willing to share their experiences and offer advice.

Veterinarians

Just as with the family cat or dog, pet box turtles should be seen by a veterinarian when first brought home and yearly thereafter. This is especially true for newly acquired wild-caught Asian box turtles. They are often sick and have large parasite loads resulting from the stresses of capture, poor diet, and long transit times from their country of origin. Long and aggressive medical intervention may be required to rid them of internal parasites or bacterial infections. All wild-caught Asian species should have a quarantine period of 12 months before joining established collections.

Find a veterinarian familiar with turtles or one who treats reptiles. Vital measurements such as weight and size should be taken and recorded. Baseline fecal tests and blood work for older animals should be performed to ascertain your pet's health. You should be asked about husbandry issues such as diet, housing, humidity, heating, and lighting. If your turtle becomes sick later, the veterinarian will then have a medical history for comparison. Depending on the legislation governing your area, he or she may also be required to sign state or federal forms to permit possession of box turtles. Some states are now requiring that transponders be implanted into native box turtles to help stop illegal collection.

It is best to take your box turtle to a reptile-specialist veterinarian for checkups yearly.

Five Ways to Find a Reptile Veterinarian

1. The Association of Reptile and Amphibian Veterinarians has a website that lists member veterinarians with a special interest in treating reptiles: www.arav.org/Directory.htm
2. Call your nearest zoo and ask to speak to the keeper in charge of reptiles. Ask him or her which veterinarians take care of their zoo herps.
3. Join a turtle club or herp society. The members may be able to recommend veterinarians who treat reptiles. You can find a list of some clubs at www.anapsid.org/societies
4. Join online communities with people from all over the world that share experience and knowledge via e-mail discussion groups. World Chelonian Trust at www.chelonia.org has an online community; others can be found at www.groups.yahoo.com.
5. Contact your state wildlife departments or local wildlife rehab groups and ask which veterinarians are called on for injured or sick reptiles. State wildlife departments can be found by contacting your state government offices.

When to See a Veterinarian

Even very fastidious and careful pet owners may have occasions when their turtle needs the expertise and assistance of a qualified reptile veterinarian. The best and most dedicated reptile veterinarians belong to the Association of Reptile and Amphibian Veterinarians, or ARAV. Members are listed on their website, www.arav.org.

Many medical issues and most invasive treatments should not be attempted by the owner. The types of medications and directions for administering them should be on the advice of your veterinarian. Your veterinarian should see your turtle yearly for routine examination and a pre-hibernation checkup and to sign off on required state or federal forms. If your turtles hibernate, late summer or early autumn is the best time to have the exam done. The veterinarian may want to perform a fecal test to check for internal parasites and run blood tests.

Box Turtle First Aid

Some of the more common and non-life threatening problems that affect box turtles can be treated by the pet owner. Assemble a first aid kit for your turtle and have it readily available in case of emergency. Certain other conditions can be treated by the more

First Signs of Illness

Abnormal behavior (e.g., pacing, soaking too much, etc.)

Anorexia

Diarrhea

Green, malodorous feces or urates

Liquid discharge from nares or mouth

Puffy eyelids or partially closed eyes

experienced turtle keepers. If you are a new owner or have any doubts, by all means consult your veterinarian immediately.

The Hospital Tank

The hospital tank is simply a small indoor terrarium that will allow the keeper to give therapeutic care and pay closer attention to a sick or injured turtle. Use a 20-gallon (76 L), 30 in. x 12 in. x 12 in. (76 cm x 30 cm x 30 cm) glass tank or a large 31-gallon (118 L) plastic container. It should be spacious enough for the turtle to be comfortable, yet small enough to control temperature and humidity. If you use a tank, cover the sides with paper so the turtle cannot see out. Use a thick clean towel as a substrate. Place shredded newspaper on one side of the tank to be used as a hide. If the turtle is not suffering from an injury, you can use moist sphagnum moss instead of the towel and shredded newspaper. Place a waterproof hide box on the moss.

Items for the Herp First Aid Kit

Adhesive stretch tape

Adhesive-coated polyurethane film dressing

Antiseptic solution such as povidone-iodine or chlorhexidine gluconate

Clean towels

Cotton-tipped swabs

Gauze pads

Jeweler's loupe to inspect wounds

Large nail clippers

Latex gloves

Sharp scissors

Small tweezers

Squeeze bottle filled with distilled water for flushing wounds or eyes

Styptic powder or corn starch to stop bleeding

Triple antibiotic ointment.

Vetwrap

Waterproof bandages of various sizes

Place a fluorescent UVB light fixture over the tank. Leave the lights on for 12 hours a day; if the sick turtle is being overwintered, keep them on for 14 hours a day. Provide a shallow water dish on the other side and change the water frequently. A heat lamp with 75-watt bulb should be placed over the water dish. Maintain the temperature at 85° F (29.4° C) on the water side and 75° F (23.9° C) on the side with the hide. If necessary, use a lower or higher wattage bulb to get the proper temperatures. A digital thermometer should be placed at the turtle's level. An infrared light bulb can be used on one side of the hospital tank if overnight temperatures fall below 75° F (23.9° C). If the turtle has an open wound, use a screen over any tank openings to prevent flies from getting in.

The newspaper bedding and towels need to be changed daily (sphagnum moss should be rinsed frequently). There is little ambient humidity in the hospital tank with newspaper bedding, so it is important to soak the turtle daily in tepid water (deep enough for the turtle to be half-submerged). If the turtle is on antibiotics, soak two times a day. Many antibiotics have by-products that are toxic to the kidneys, so ample hydration is necessary to aid in eliminating the toxins.

Superficial Wounds

Examine your turtle often, especially if it lives outdoors or in a communal enclosure. Turtles, especially rival males and both sexes of the aggressive aquatic Asian species, can bite and scratch each other. Minor cuts on the skin and shell can be treated with your first aid kit. Clean cuts on the skin or the shell thoroughly with a disinfectant like chlorhexidine gluconate or a dilute povidone-iodine solution (1:10 dilution with water). Examine the cut with a magnifying glass to see whether debris is embedded in the wound. Protect the area with gauze and tape (vetwrap, Band-Aid, or New Skin). If the cut is large, place the outdoor turtle in a screened-over hospital tank to prevent flies from laying eggs in the

Examine your box turtle daily for signs of illness. This is a yellow-margined box turtle.

The Five Most Common Illnesses That Require Veterinary Care

1. Eye infections: caused by bacteria or vitamin A (retinol) deficiency
2. Internal parasites: caused by various organisms
3. Middle ear abscess: bacterial infection caused by poor husbandry
4. Shell rot: bacterial or fungal infections caused by poor husbandry
5. Upper respiratory infection: caused by bacteria or viruses when immunity is depressed

wound. Apply a thin layer of triple antibiotic ointment to any wound that becomes red or will not heal. Clean daily and apply ointment until healing is complete. If the cuts are deep or caused by dog or cat bites, take the turtle to a veterinarian.

External Parasites

Turtles living outside will come into contact with invertebrates, some of which are external parasites (ectoparasites) that prey upon turtles. Chiggers, mites, ticks, fly larvae, leeches, mosquitoes, and other parasites as well as fire ants and wasp can cause box turtles considerable distress. Of most concern is the ability of some parasites to transmit viral or bacterial diseases to their hosts. Mosquitoes attack the head, eyes, vent, and scute margins by feeding on the host's blood, a process by which diseases can be transmitted.

Fire ants (*Solenopsis invicta*) are especially dangerous to turtles and other ground- dwelling animals. These non-native pests have killed many hatchlings and even adults. Box turtles close up in their shells and become immobile when threatened, but this allows the fire ants to swarm over the hapless victims. Follow the actions described in the housing chapter to eradicate these pests before they bother your pets.

Aquatic turtles can come into contact with leeches if housed outside and should be checked regularly. Indoor turtle pets are not necessarily safe from ectoparasites, as these pests can be introduced via other pets or cage furnishings (such as logs or rocks).

Mites and Ticks Mite infestation is usually not a problem with outdoor enclosures. If you notice mites, turn over the soil and let it dry for a few days before adding a new layer of topsoil. Indoor mite infestation can become a serious problem, especially if you also keep snakes or lizards. If you have an infestation of snake mites (*Ophionyssus natricis)*, remove and replace the bedding and any live plants. Thoroughly clean the tank and all furnishings, including plastic plants, tank hood, hide boxes, and water bowls by using scalding hot water and soap. The mites lay eggs on cage furnishings, so repeat this process several times a week for as long as necessary to remove all mites.

Mites appear as tiny dark specks massed around the eyes or on the skin. Scrub the turtle shell and accessible body parts with a soft toothbrush and a mixture of warm water and an antiseptic solution. You may need to wash a turtle several times to remove the mites. Treat areas around the eyes by covering them with a thin layer of ophthalmic antibiotic ointment. If you decide to use a commercial miticide, use one that is safe for chelonians. Miticides made with permethrins and permectrins are generally safe for turtles. Miticides containing ivermectin are extremely dangerous and potentially fatal to turtles and should never be used. Products containing organophosphates are potentially toxic and could harm turtles if used incorrectly, or on immature or small specimens. Follow the manufacturer's directions when using any kind of pesticide.

Box turtles housed outdoors are at risk of contracting parasites. A Chinese three-striped box turtle is shown.

Ticks and leeches attach themselves to the skin of turtles with their mouthparts. Check your turtles regularly for these pests, especially under the legs and neck. A tick's connection is strong, but the parasite can be removed with steady pressure. Use your fingers or tick removers to grasp the thorax, (body part behind the head and above the abdomen) and pull the tick straight out. Check to see whether the tick's head is still attached to its body. If the head remains in the skin of the turtle, an infection may develop. Take your turtle to a veterinarian if this happens.

Blowfly and Botfly Box turtles are commonly parasitized by two types of flies. One is the botfly. It lays its eggs on the turtle's skin, usually on the neck or legs. The eggs hatch and the larvae chew holes into the skin of the turtle. Under the skin, they begin to eat flesh and grow in size. The result is a swelling or lump that can be seen on the skin. Often a small opening can be seen at the apex of the lump. When the larvae are ready to pupate they emerge from the opening, drop to the ground, pupate and become flies to start the cycle over again with another host. As many as a dozen or more larvae can be removed from the lumps.

Some experienced keepers cut the lumps open themselves, but it is best to have a veterinarian remove the botfly larvae. The veterinarian will place an anesthetic cream (usually lidocaine cream) on the area to reduce pain from the incision and then flush out the larvae with a povidone-iodine solution. Antibiotic ointment may also be used to combat secondary infection.

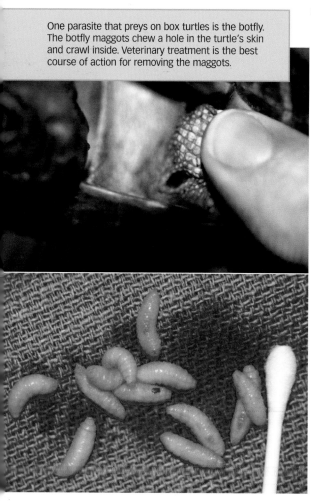

One parasite that preys on box turtles is the botfly. The botfly maggots chew a hole in the turtle's skin and crawl inside. Veterinary treatment is the best course of action for removing the maggots.

Box turtles can also fall victim to blowflies and flesh flies such as *Lucilia sericata* and *Cistudinomyia cistudinis*. These flies can smell blood and necrotic flesh and will quickly lay dozens of eggs on any open wound. After hatching, the growing maggots eat large amounts of flesh. This condition in turtles is commonly known as myiasis, or fly strike, and the afflicted animal can die from loss of blood and mass. It is extremely important that injured box turtles be kept in hospital tanks equipped with screened tops to protect them from flies.

Irregular Shell Growth

An adult box turtle's growth is minuscule each year, thus making it difficult to detect shell deformities. However, box turtles that are actively growing may quickly acquire severe shell deformities if proper diet, humidity levels, and full-spectrum

Box turtles that are fed insufficient calcium or not given access to UV light will develop abnormal shells; an extreme case is shown here next to a normal-sized shell (although this shell has shell rot).

lights are not provided. Inadequate UVB exposure, deficiencies in vitamin D3, calcium, and other nutrients, or diseased organs can cause metabolic bone disease (MBD). Turtles with MBD have shells that are either soft or easily depressed inward. In time, organs begin to fail.

Turtles with MBD have drastically decreased life spans compared to turtles that receive proper care. Turtles should be given access to natural sunlight or full-spectrum light bulbs. Keepers in colder climates can usually find times during the warmer months to provide temporary outside housing. A secure daytime pen can be made for short jaunts outdoors for sun and exercise. If natural sunlight is not available, the turtle should be given a calcium supplement that also contains vitamin D3. The turtle should also be housed under UVB lights. Adequate lighting and a suitable diet throughout the turtle's life are the best prevention for MBD.

Low humidity within the enclosure and excessive protein consumption are factors linked to pyramiding of the scutes, thickening of the shell, and curling of the marginal scutes. If you notice these symptoms, it is important to re-evaluate the diet and housing conditions. Shell deformities are a signal that the turtle keeper is doing something wrong!

Overgrown Claws and Beak

The beak and claws of a turtle are made of keratin and continue to grow throughout the turtle's life. Wild box turtles walk over rough surfaces, forage on tough plants, tear tissues off bones, and naturally wear down their claws and beaks. Turtles kept in captivity do not always get enough of this natural abrasion. Some develop misshapen jaws and end up having difficulties with eating. It is important for owners to keep claws and beaks trimmed to manageable lengths. Giving your turtle whole prey foods once a month is a good idea—chewing on bits of bones will wear down the beak, and the organs contain extra nutrients. Providing cuttlebone is another good means for keeping beaks trimmed. Create feeding substrates that are abrasive by using flat hard rocks or tile pavers.

Novices should not trim overgrown beaks until they have first observed a demonstration from their veterinarian. Trimming should be done only with a high-speed rotary file. Overgrown beaks are often very thick and dry and can crack if clippers are used. Severe injuries can occur if the crack extends through the palate or nasal passage. If this happens, the turtle should be seen by a veterinarian immediately. He may have to wire the break together and apply a layer of fiberglass or methylmethacrylate over the crack to stabilize it.

Very long claws can get stuck in cracks and be ripped off along with a toe. Turtles are unable to walk properly in severe cases. Claws can be kept short by providing access to rough surfaces during exercise or by trimming them with clippers or a high-speed rotary file. Nails that are unhealthy, dry and brittle should be trimmed with a rotary file only. Nail clippers can cause the nail to break at the base and result in profuse bleeding and infections.

Overgrown beaks should be treated by a veterinarian. Prevent this condition by giving your box turtles cuttlebone to chew.

Be sure to avoid cutting into the quick. The quick portion of the nail will be opaque when seen with a strong backlight. If you cut the quick, the turtle will feel pain and blood will seep out of the nail. Stop the bleeding with styptic powder if this happens. Longer nails typically have a longer quick as well. In such cases, trim as much of the nail as possible without damaging the quick. In a few weeks trim the nail again and repeat the process until a better length is achieved.

Off Feed

Box turtles are notorious for refusing to eat. They may become picky eaters, or even anorexic, for various reasons. Some causes are medical, but most are husbandry related. Box turtles need to be comfortable, feel safe, and recognize the food as something edible. Without a healthy appetite for nutritious foods, a turtle will succumb to a host of deficiencies and illnesses. Avoid feeding problems by evaluating and correcting any care issues that are under your control. Seek veterinarian treatment if the problems persist.

Turtle's Eyes Are Closed Turtles will not eat if their eyes are closed. Eyes that are shut and sunken in might result from a lack of humidity or poor hydration. Soak the turtle in warm water no deeper than halfway up the shell. If the eyes reopen, increase humidity and provide more or easier access to clean drinking water and soaking opportunities. Check the humidity and temperature at the turtle's level in the enclosure using an accurate digital thermometer and hygrometer, which are available at electronics stores and some pet shops. In order to digest food properly, core body temperatures for box turtles must be in the range of 75° to 80° F (24° to 27° C), depending on the species.

If the problem persists, check to see whether the substrate material is causing eye irritation. Do not use cedar or pine bedding, because they release irritating aromatic

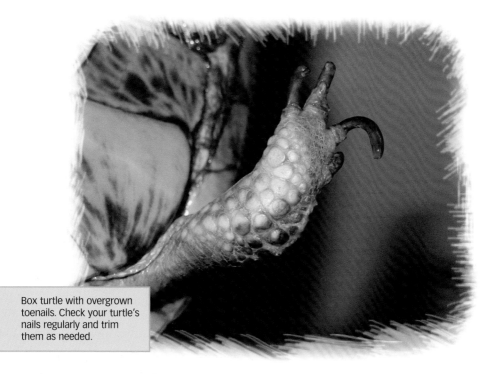

Box turtle with overgrown toenails. Check your turtle's nails regularly and trim them as needed.

chemicals and can cause long-term liver damage. Aquatic box turtles are sensitive to dirty water. Along with adequate filtration, regular water changes should be performed to keep the water clear and the pH between 6 and 7. Some eye conditions are associated with respiratory infections or vitamin A deficiency and require immediate veterinarian care.

Turtle Suddenly Stops Eating Colder weather in the fall and winter will cause turtles to stop eating. Cooler temperatures and reduced hours of sunlight are their signals to begin hibernation. Even indoor turtles living in controlled environments will notice the change in the season and may begin to eat less. To prevent this, increase the temperature and humidity to summer-like conditions and adjust the duration of both light sources (heat and UVB) to 14 hours a day. Provide as much live food as possible throughout the winter to keep appetites stimulated. Turtles can become bored with food items just as humans do. Follow the meal plan laid out in the diet chapter and use a variety of foods.

New Turtle Won't Eat A new turtle can be stressed and may not eat initially. New turtles should be taken to a veterinarian as soon as possible to rule out any medical problems. Once back home, give the turtle time to acclimate. You can leave food under a ledge or bush if the turtle is outside. Put the food down, then walk away and allow it to eat in peace. If housed inside, cut a door on the side of a small box and put a plate of food inside so the turtle will feel secure while eating. Sometimes patiently holding a piece of boiled chicken in front of the turtle's face will entice it to take a nip.

Vitamin and Mineral Deficiencies

Box turtles need a variety of vitamins and minerals including calcium; vitamins A, D3, C, and vitamin B complex; magnesium; selenium; and iodine. Most of these are supplied naturally in a fresh, omnivorous diet. Foods such as whole prey, high-quality protein, fresh vegetables, fruits, and specialty turtle and tortoise chows can supply these nutrients. You can also use a high-quality vitamin preparation once a week for added insurance. Put pieces of cuttlebone in the pen for chewing and added calcium, especially when you have gravid females. Calcium supplements should not contain added phosphorus, as the omnivorous diet already supplies plenty of that mineral. The ratio of calcium to phosphorus in the diet should be maintained at 2 to 1.

Gut Impaction

A distressful ailment in turtles is gut impaction. A turtle that has not had a bowel movement for a week or one that appears to strain when defecating may have an obstruction in the intestines. This is different from constipation, although frequent bouts of constipation can lead to impactions. Indigestible material is usually the cause, but the problem may also result from parasite infestations. Parasitic worms can perforate the intestines, making it important to see a veterinarian immediately.

Obstructions are often caused by accidental ingestion of bedding or pebbles or from

Not Dead Yet

If you discover a seemingly dead turtle submerged in water, remember that these animals can withstand oxygen deprivation much longer than mammals or birds. You may in fact be able to resuscitate it. Tilt the turtle's head down while pushing its hind legs in and out, helping to expel water out of the lungs and pulling air back into them. Continue working the legs for at least fifteen minutes before giving up.

eating insects with hard exoskeletons. Cold enclosures can limit the turtle's ability to have active intestinal contractions. Whatever the cause, infrequent or strained bowel movements will lead to bigger problems. Impacted turtles are more susceptible to having prolapsed organs.

If suspected, soak the turtle in tepid water (deep enough to immerse the cloaca) several times a day for a few days. Try putting a few drops of salad oil or vitamin E oil on a favorite food or directly into the mouth with an eyedropper. Or you can use a feline hairball remover, which will bind to the foreign material and pass it through the gut. If home care fails to produce a bowel movement within a week, take the turtle to a veterinarian.

Avoid impactions by feeding the turtle on a hard flat surface instead of directly off the bedding. I feed my turtles on clay floor tiles. A few messy eaters have to be fed on large plastic plant saucers. If you see your turtle attempting to eat pebbles, provide more cuttlebone or a mineral block made for birds. It is interesting that X-rays of wild box turtles show incidents of small pebbles in their stomach and

Feeding your box turtle directly on the substrate can lead to gut impactions. It is best to feed your turtle on a plate or something similar.

intestines. Whether intentional or not, it appears that having some pebbles in the gut is normal. The danger occurs when gut mobility is limited due to cold temperatures, lack of exercise, or lack of fiber in the diet.

Serious Health Issues

Of course, not every illness or injury a box turtle might get is treatable by the keeper. The health conditions covered in this section are serious and warrant a visit to a veterinarian as soon as symptoms appear.

Respiratory Infection

Box turtles with reduced immunity are susceptible to respiratory infections (also called runny nose syndrome or RNS) that cause discharge from the nares and mouth. In severe cases, infection in the lungs can lead to pneumonia. Many opportunistic bacteria and viruses cause respiratory infections in box turtles. Symptoms will include labored or open-mouth breathing with discharge of mucus from the mouth and nares and bubbly, squeaking, or raspy sounds from the lungs. If the sick turtle is housed outside, bring it indoors and use a hospital tank. Sick turtles should immediately be separated from other turtles to minimize the spread of RNS. Because of the threat of pneumonia, see a veterinarian immediately.

Some veterinarians may collect a culture swab from the nares to determine which antibiotics will work best. In most cases the veterinarian will prescribe a broad-spectrum antibiotic, such as enrofloxacin or ceftazidime. While on antibiotics, the turtle should be soaked in tepid water a few times a day for up to a week after the last shot. This helps remove the toxic byproducts of antibiotic therapy that could cause secondary renal damage if not flushed from the body with good hydration.

Mycoplasma agassizii is a bacterium that causes upper respiratory tract disease, or URTD, and was first found in desert tortoises. A similar disease is found in box turtles; it is marked by excessive nasal discharge, swollen eyelids, and anorexia. Although a turtle can recover with antibiotic

Typhoid Mary Turtle

Never release pet turtles back into the wild. Even if they appear healthy, they can still be carriers of viruses or bacteria that can decimate native turtle populations. *Mycoplasma agassizii* is a bacterium that has killed many native desert tortoises through contact with infected pet tortoises that were released by their owners.

treatment and home care, it is never rid of the disease agent. Poor diet or improper housing can weaken its immunity and allow URTD to resurface.

Turtles with respiratory infections will not eat and may become anorexic. On the advice of your veterinarian, the turtle may need to be force-fed by stomach tube. The veterinarian should perform the procedure the first few times and train you in how to avoid aspiration of food into the lungs but may prefer to perform the procedure for the course of the illness, depending on the recovery time. Liquid foods made especially for omnivorous reptiles are now available and are useful for long-term nutritional support. If assisted feeding must be performed for more than a few weeks, an esophagostomy tube—a tube surgically inserted into the esophagus—can be used. Advantages of this procedure are the lessened risk of damage or aspiration and elimination of the stress of having the turtle's mouth forced open.

Box turtles sometimes get clear bubbly discharge from the nose that is not necessarily caused by a bacterial or viral infection. Cold temperatures, low humidity, dusty bedding, and even internal parasites can cause runny noses. A veterinarian can help you pin-point the cause of runny nose syndrome (RNS).

Viral Infections

As turtles and tortoises are bred in ever larger numbers at zoos, at breeding facilities, and by hobbyists, more cases of viral infections are being observed in chelonian populations. One example of a viral contagion is the herpes virus. It afflicts the green sea turtle (*Chelonia mydas*), causing lesions and tumors on the body and within internal organs. Although the etiology of the virus is not known, the head start of hatchlings in large communal pools may have inadvertently spread the virus to more turtles than would have otherwise been exposed. Unexplained illnesses that have swept through box turtle collections may be caused by similar viral agents. If you have a large collection of turtles, do not keep them all in one large pen. If a viral outbreak should occur, separate housing may help prevent spreading of the disease. Never mix species such as *Cuora* and *Terrapene* in the same enclosure. Some species may have immunities to diseases that are deadly to others.

Septicemic Cutaneous Ulcerative Disease (SCUD)

Shell rot (SCUD) is a serious disease that can cause permanent damage to the shell and lead to systemic infection if not controlled at the onset of symptoms. Shell rot is caused by opportunistic pathogens. The key word for the keeper is *opportunistic*. The owner must be vigilant for any lapses in husbandry, especially dirty conditions, which can suppress the turtle's immune system and provide a breeding ground for bacteria and fungi. For example, if the aquatic Malayan and Chinese three-striped turtles are kept in dry conditions their shells may dry out and become flaky. This will provide sites where bacteria or fungi can take harbor and multiply. Clean any scratches or cuts in the shell with antibacterial soap and always be on the lookout for signs of shell rot.

Bacterial infections cause "wet" shell rot, whereas fungal problems cause "dry" shell rot. Both can be present at the same time. Signs of wet shell rot are soft or loose scutes and a foul smell around the area. Dry shell rot will cause areas of the shell to look pitted, flaky, and whitish as the fungi eat away at the keratin. Once the rot begins, it can spread and cause damage to larger areas. If left unchecked, shell rot can penetrate into the body of the turtle and cause septicemia or a systemic infection.

Take the turtle to a veterinarian right away, because the problem might be more extensive than what is visible on the shell. The veterinarian may want to perform cytology on the debris and make cultures to determine the underlying cause. The results of these tests will determine the appropriate medication and can clue you in on the husbandry issues that need attention.

Treatment for shell rot is often complex, especially if not addressed early. The veterinarian will initially remove loose shell and dead tissue, then thoroughly clean all affected areas. Antibiotics or antifungal cream are prescribed, depending on the type of infection. It can take many weeks to clear up the infection, and you may be asked to do the follow-up work. This involves inspecting the shell for new signs of rot, removing loose shell or necrotic tissue, cleaning the area with an antibacterial solution and a soft toothbrush, and applying the medication. During this time, keep the turtle in a hospital tank to aid in keeping the wounds clean. Aquatic box turtles can be kept in a "clean" aquarium with no substrate, water temperatures of 80° to 84° F (27° to 28° C), and a substrate-free haul-out platform. A heat lamp should maintain the basking area at 85° to 89° F (30° to 32° C), and there should be a UVB light bulb overhead.

A box turtle suffering from shell rot. This serious condition is caused by infections related to poor husbandry or predator bites.

Aural Abscess

Lumps that appear on one or both sides of a turtle's head may be a symptom of middle ear infections. When an infection occurs here, the tympanic scale bulges out from the build-up of caseous pus within the canal—turtles and other reptiles lack the enzyme to liquefy the pus. A cheesy-looking white substance may be visible if the aural abscess has ruptured.

These abscesses can become quite large and cause the turtle significant discomfort. Veterinary care is urgently required. Although systemic antibiotics may help if the problem is caught early, most cases require a surgical procedure on the abscess. Topical anesthetics, or preferably general anesthesia, should be applied before lancing. The veterinarian will make an incision across the tympanic scale and remove the caseous pus by flushing the canal with sterile saline or an antiseptic solution. In most cases the wound is left open for drainage. Antibiotics may be prescribed. Following surgery, the turtle should be housed in a hospital tank until it becomes active again. Bacteria of the genus *Pseudomonas* have been cultured from aural abscesses, but often the pus is not laden with bacteria. No single bacterial agent has been found responsible for aural abscesses. It is likely that the bacteria are not the primary cause, but simply opportunistic pathogens.

They can occur when indoor or outdoor turtles are kept in cold, damp conditions. Low-grade respiratory infections can cause a backup of infectious debris that impacts the eustachian tubes, thereby causing middle ear infections. Very dry conditions can also cause ear abscesses,

Aural abscesses in box turtles are often caused by inappropriate temperatures or vitamin A deficiency.

as can organochlorine-induced vitamin A deficiencies. Turtles kept in appropriate housing and fed a proper diet are more likely to have a strong immune system and can fight off such infections.

Eye Infections

Another common problem in turtles with a history of poor husbandry or declining health is the accumulation of pus under the eyelids and over the corneal surface. The Harderian glands in the eyes are susceptible to inadequate levels of vitamin A. The deficiency causes Harderian secretions to be reduced, leading to conjunctivitis and thick pus accumulation. The pus is hard and should be removed by a veterinarian. The process involves long soaks in tepid water and application of a softening agent to loosen the pus. Slight pressure is applied to the lower eyelids and the pus expelled. Antibiotic eye ointment is applied several times a day for several weeks.

Not every case of conjunctivitis is caused from a deficiency of vitamin A—sometimes it results from too much! Vitamin A toxicity (overdose, also called hypervitaminosis A) also manifests with swollen eyes, as well as skin sloughing and lesions or redness on the limbs. A thorough history of the turtle's diet and health is required before making a proper diagnosis. Vitamin A is fat soluble and can be stored in the turtle's body, where it can reach toxic levels. Injections of this supplement should only be given by an experienced reptile veterinarian, and only after careful diagnosis. A safer means of providing additional vitamin A is by dietary changes (see chapter on diet).

Five Signs Your Turtle May be in Pain

1. Aggression
2. Anorexia
3. Protection of painful sites
4. Reluctance to move
5. Stiffness, lameness

Other conditions of the eyes include tumors, ulcerations, injuries, and freeze damage. All problems associated with the eyes should be seen by a veterinarian. Blind turtles do thrive, but only when the owner is willing to hand feed and provide other special care.

Nutritional Diseases

A turtle that does not receive adequate nutrition can suffer from various nutritional diseases. These problems can be avoided if the captive diet follows the instructions found in the diet chapter. However, an affected turtle may have a past history of poor diet and may only now be displaying symptoms of vitamin A, vitamin D3, or calcium deficiencies. These turtles may be anorexic, have swollen eyelids, conjunctivitis, and/or soft shells. It may be difficult to diagnose a nutritional disease unless the life history is known. If you suspect this to be the case, take your turtle to a veterinarian for assessment and nutritional treatment.

Starvation

A long-standing illness, severe injury, or poor husbandry can lead to starvation. A turtle may stop eating and eventually waste away body mass. If you receive a turtle that is light in weight and not eating, take it to your veterinarian immediately. In many cases the turtle will require enteral feedings by means of a stomach tube or via an esophagostomy tube. Enteral nutrition provides adequate calories from proteins, fats, carbohydrates, and amino acids in a form that is easy to digest. Debilitated turtles do not have sufficient reserves of energy needed to process regular whole foods. As soon as the turtle begins to eat on its own, try dipping food in jarred baby food vegetables or meats. Gradually increase portions and offerings until it is eating a complete meal.

Internal Parasites

Common internal parasites in box turtles are worms (nematodes, cestodes, and trematodes) and protozoans. Most box turtles will have internal worms sometime during their lives. They may become infected by ingesting feces-contaminated soil that contains the eggs or cysts of direct life cycle parasites (e.g. ascarids, pinworms, and hookworms). Turtles can also get internal parasites by eating earthworms, snails, or other intermediate hosts that are infected with the larvae of tapeworms, flukes, and other indirect life cycle parasites.

Worms Some worms can be seen by the naked eye. Actively look for them whenever you change the turtle's water or observe fresh stools. Most internal parasites cannot be seen without magnification—routine screening should be done twice a year. If the turtle becomes listless, anorexic, foams at the mouth, stops defecating, or regurgitates food, it should be seen by a veterinarian immediately. Large parasitic loads can cause gut impaction or perforate the intestines, leading to damage of the liver, kidney, lungs, or heart. The prognosis is not good in these cases. The veterinarian will identify the type of worms afflicting your pet and prescribe a deworming medication. You will be asked to return for a follow-up test to determine whether a second round of deworming is necessary.

Turtles should never be given dewormers unless the veterinarian is certain the medication will not have adverse effects. Several mammal dewormers cause death in turtles and should never be used. Two of these are ivermectin and piperazine; others may also be toxic. Safer products include pyrantel pamoate, which is effective against numerous parasitic worms, and praziquantal for tapeworms. Even these products may not be safe for debilitated turtles and should never be used without veterinary assistance. Fenbendazole, used to treat roundworms, has recently come under scrutiny regarding its safety and proper dosages for box turtles.

Protozoans Protozoans are another group of internal parasites affecting turtles. They are single-celled organisms that cause considerable damage for their size! Protozoans of the genus *Hexamita* and some in the order Coccidia are highly contagious pathogens that are increasingly being observed in box turtles. Symptoms of *Hexamita* infection are dark green strong-smelling urine, anorexia, and fluid retention. If left untreated, these protozoans will ascend from the bladder into the kidneys, causing permanent damage and death. Turtles infected with coccidiosis will have severe diarrhea.

Eye inflammations in box turtles can result from too much or too little vitamin A. This turtle has healthy eyes

Parasite Lifestyle: Direct vs. Indirect

The terms direct and indirect describe two different ways parasites infect their hosts. In a direct lifestyle, the parasite needs only the host and can repeatedly infest the same individual and others sharing the same habitat. For example, hookworms have a direct life cycle and can grow, reproduce, and shed eggs in the feces of its host. In unsanitary conditions, an otherwise healthy turtle may pick up worms from eating feces-contaminated food or soil. Parasites with an indirect life cycle need to spend time in an intermediate host, such as a snail, before moving on to the final host where they grow and reproduce.

Change the tank substrate regularly and remove feces often to prevent direct contact with worm eggs. Regularly clean and disinfect dishes and other pen furnishings that might come into contact with feces.

Prompt medical intervention is needed to treat these illnesses. Metronidazole (usually available under the brand name Flagyl) is often used against protozoal illnesses.

Turtles under stress are more susceptible to protozoal illnesses. Wild-caught Asian box turtles usually endure high-stress conditions and should be checked for these parasites. A deadly protozoan common in many is *Entamoeba*. Carriers may be asymptomatic but can infect other turtles, resulting in mass die-offs. This is yet another reason why different species of turtles should never be housed in mixed groups.

Necrotic Stomatitis (Mouth Rot)

Debilitated turtles and those that have had a prolonged illness can succumb to fungi and bacteria that cause mouth rot. Some turtles coming out of hibernation may present with mouth rot, suggesting they were not healthy going in. *Never allow sickly or underweight turtles to go into hibernation.*

Check for mouth rot by holding the head firmly behind the jaws and use the eraser end of a pencil to push down on the lower jaw. The irritated turtle will try to bite the eraser, giving you a chance to look into the mouth. Fungal mouth rot will look like a cheesy white growth and sometimes hardened pus and dead tissue on the tongue or palate. Bacterial mouth rot can cause the formation of red or black blisters. Take the turtle to a veterinarian immediately If you suspect mouth rot. A scraping from the turtle's mouth and inspection under a microscope may be necessary to determine the nature of the infection. Antifungal or antibiotic medications may be prescribed, depending on the findings. Maintaining a healthy immune system is the best way to keep ever-present opportunistic pathogens from affecting your turtle.

Wild-caught Asian box turtles, such as yellow-margined box turtles, frequently carry protozoan parasites.

Diarrhea

Diarrhea is a warning sign of a medical or husbandry problem in any animal and should never be ignored. Turtle feces should be firm and dark in color and have very little odor. Review the current diet of any turtle that has diarrhea. Are too many watery foods with little fiber content being used? If the stools are odorous, greenish, and watery, the turtle should be taken to a reptile veterinarian immediately. Testing will pinpoint the problem and proper medication can be prescribed. All turtles with diarrhea should be housed separately in hospital tanks. It is not uncommon for turtles to have *Salmonella*, *Enterobacter*, or *Escherichia coli*, all of which can be transmitted to humans—use special caution to avoid contamination.

Dehydration

Mild cases of dehydration are common in box turtles. Turtles need clean water daily for drinking and soaking. Illnesses that cause diarrhea may cause dehydration. In serious cases of dehydration, the turtle will have sunken eyes, dry flaky skin, tacky mucous membranes, weight loss, and thick ropy saliva.

A severely dehydrated turtle should be seen by a veterinarian who will provide subcutaneous hydration that furnishes water as well as replaces lost electrolytes. A check for secondary medical problems will also be given. Severe dehydration causes organ failure. Renal dysfunction and subsequent renal failure can occur when bodily by-products like uric acid accumulate in the kidneys. Secondary infections can develop as the turtle's immune system becomes compromised. Always provide clean water in a large shallow dish that is easy for the turtle to enter and leave. Place the dehydrated turtle in the water dish a few times a day for a week, or until it readily enters the dish on its own.

Paralyzed Limbs

A mysterious ailment that occurs in some box turtles is the onset of paralysis in the legs. It usually starts in one limb and may eventually progress to all four. The cause of the paralysis is unknown, and many times the turtle recovers. Unfortunately, the condition can be permanent—the turtle may languish in this fashion for years before dying.

Paralysis is likely a symptom of several different diseases. One such disease may be a viral infection that causes muscle, nerve, or brain damage. Another might be spinal pressure from abnormal shell or bone growth, or nutritional deficiencies that affect the nerves or muscles. In most cases, veterinarians cannot make a diagnosis unless the owner can provide an accurate life history of the turtle. Therefore good records are vital; they should include the turtle's age, medical history, and other information that might be useful. Make note of any bad falls or possible consumption of contaminated plants or insects. Other illnesses that affect limb mobility include gout, bone or joint infections, and septic arthritis. These are treatable conditions and a veterinarian should be consulted.

All box turtles need access to water for soaking and drinking. This three-toed box turtle is drinking from the artificial stream in its enclosure.

Dystocia (Egg Binding)

Dystocia is a condition in which a female turtle cannot deposit her eggs. If you notice a female pacing, frequently soaking, weak in her hind limbs, straining, constipated, fasting, or otherwise behaving abnormally for more than one week, seek veterinary care. This is a serious problem that requires expert attention.

The veterinarian will take a radiograph (X-ray) to determine whether egg binding is present. Treatment may involve anesthetizing the turtle in order to break down the ova and remove them through the cloaca. In a number of cases, successful surgeries have been performed in which the plastron was cut open, the oviducts exposed, and the impacted eggs removed. Another treatment attempts to induce egg expulsion with injections of calcium borogluconate and the hormone oxytocin. Caution is advised in the use of oxytocin: it produces strong contractions along the oviduct walls and can crush eggs that cannot pass because of shell deformities. If egg binding is not treated, the ova could become crushed within the body—the decaying mass will most likely lead to peritonitis (inflammation of the abdominal wall). Breeding-age females can lay infertile eggs and should always be provided areas suitable for nesting whether males are present or not.

Prolapsed Organs

Box turtles have only one vent, the cloaca. All eliminations, as well as eggs, come out of the body through this opening. Internal organs are sometimes extruded from the cloaca. The intestines, oviduct, stomach, bladder, and the cloaca itself are capable of prolapsing. A prolapsed organ cannot be withdrawn into the cloaca and is dragged behind the turtle as it walks. This is an *emergency* situation requiring immediate veterinary care. In such cases, the turtles have often been victims of poor husbandry and diet. Extremely sick turtles or those with a history of frequent constipation and impaction are susceptible to prolapsed organs.

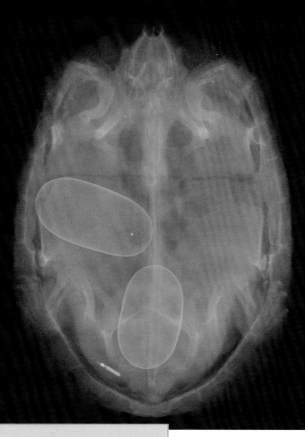

If you suspect your turtle is egg-bound, take it to a vet for an x-ray. This Asian box turtle has two eggs developing.

Male box turtles will sometimes evert their genitals from the cloaca in a behavior called "penis fanning." An owner unfamiliar with the behavior may think something is wrong. However, it is normal and nothing to be alarmed about as long as the genitals can be withdrawn back into the body within a few minutes. Penis fanning begins with the male standing tall on his hind limbs, straining to push out his genital organ, which unfurls from the cloaca like a blossoming flower. It is dark purple, plump from blood, and is large compared to the size of the cloaca. Sometimes it cannot be withdrawn back into the body. If this occurs, the turtle should be placed in a hospital tank lined with very wet towels to help keep the genitals moist. Apply a thin layer of hemorrhoid ointment to the organ to help reduce swelling. Soaking the turtle in sugar water or corn syrup may help with shrinkage and retraction. Take the turtle to a reptile veterinarian if the organ does not retract into the cloaca within a few hours. Your veterinarian can use a variety of techniques to remedy the problem and may prescribe follow-up care. In cases of severe damage or infection, the penis must be amputated.

Animal Attack

Dogs, raccoons, coyotes, and rats, as well as ravens and chipmunks, have all been linked to box turtle deaths. It is imperative that owners do everything in their power to protect pet turtles from dogs and other animals. Even the well-trained family pet dog has a natural instinct to chew things, and a turtle looks just as good as a large meat bone! If your turtle is

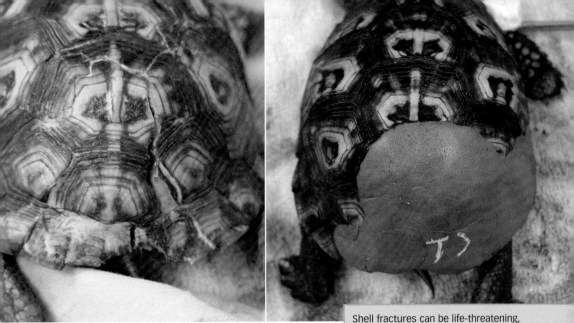

Shell fractures can be life-threatening, so seek prompt veterinary attention if this occurs to your turtle. Your vet will repair the fracture with an epoxy and probably prescribe antibiotics.

ever bitten by an animal, take it to a veterinarian. A small bite on the skin or a piece broken from the shell could lead to massive infection or shell rot if not thoroughly cleaned and medicated. Some turtles require limb amputation because of damage or infection. These pets can still lead normal lives—please consider treatment rather than euthanasia.

Shell Fractures

Shell fractures require immediate attention by a veterinarian. Lung and coelomic organ exposure through the fracture sites are a crisis situation requiring immediate aggressive veterinary treatment. Even less serious fractures can be life-threatening, because bacteria can enter the cracks and cause septicemia. Septicemia is a body-wide infection that can cause organ failure and death. One of the symptoms is a reddening of the plastron as blood begins to pool in the lower extremities. The limbs may swell as the kidneys shut down, and the turtle will become listless and anorexic. Once the turtle is at this stage, death almost invariably occurs. Prevent fractures by keeping your turtle away from mowers and other sources of danger.

A reptile veterinarian may be able to repair a fractured shell using a combination of bone screws, wire, and medical-grade epoxy cement. In the past, a covering of fiberglass would be applied over the cracks to form a hard shell. Newer procedures call for covering the shell with sterile adhesive vetwrap. This will allow the crack to be regularly cleaned and examined, and given secondary treatments as needed. Incredible shell repairs leading to full recoveries have been performed by veterinarians.

Zoonoses

Many types of bacteria, viruses, and parasites can be transferred to pet owners and anyone else coming into contact with an infected turtle, its feces, or any of the enclosure contents. A keeper merely needs to practice good hygiene and thorough hand washing to eliminate chances of contracting zoonoses (diseases that can pass from animals to people).

Good hygiene requires that the kitchen sink be off limits to the turtle and any of its dishes, soaking bowls, or cage materials. Everything the turtle touches should be cleaned outdoors or in a bathroom basin or tub. Once a basin or tub has been used, it should be sprayed with a weak solution of bleach (1 part bleach to 9 parts water), let sit for 5 to 10 minutes, then rinsed well and washed again with hot soapy water. Clean the water bowls and food dishes in the same manner. If you wash and reuse bedding, rinse it several times with hot water until the draining water is clear. Keep the turtle's environment clean and you will reduce the possibility of contamination.

Avoiding Salmonella

Salmonella bacteria pass from infected feces to new victims via oral and nasal pathways. Avoid touching your mouth, nose, and eyes with dirty hands. Anyone who handles a turtle should wash their hands with antibacterial soap immediately afterward. Never eat, drink, or smoke when handling your turtle or cleaning its enclosure.

Salmonella

Salmonella is a genus of bacteria that has been found in pigs, chickens and their eggs, unpasteurized milk and orange juice, frogs, turtles, lettuce, and many other animals and plants. *Salmonella* causes gastrointestinal distress including diarrhea, abdominal cramps, fever, nausea, and vomiting in humans. Although not all box turtles carry *Salmonella*, every reptile should be assumed to be a carrier. Death from salmonellosis (the term for infection with *Salmonella*) is uncommon, but people with HIV/AIDS or other immuno-deficient disorders, or who take anti-rejection drugs, the elderly, the very young, and pregnant women should not risk contamination by handling reptiles of any kind. Stringent hygiene practices will reduce chances of getting salmonellosis.

Euthanasia

Putting down a sick or injured pet is never easy, but sometimes it is the kindest thing a person can do for a suffering animal. In the case of box turtles, it is hard to know when suffering occurs. They have no voice, nor do they shiver or cry. If your veterinarian is fully aware of the extent of the disease or injury, he or she may be your best guide. If you have doubts, get a second opinion. Good veterinarians will respect your choice to do so.

Turtles are remarkably resilient. When hit by a car or lawn mower, they often make full recoveries with only damaged shells as a reminder of their injuries. Each turtle is a unique and precious individual and deserves the chance to recover. However, when one must be put down, ask a veterinarian to euthanize it humanely. Freezing a turtle to death is inhumane. Ice crystals forming in the skin cause pain and distress before brain death occurs. Poisoning, decapitating, asphyxiating, or crushing are inappropriate methods and certainly not painless.

To prevent salmonellosis and other diseases, always wash your hands after handling your turtle or its cage fixtures.

To achieve a painless death, the animal should be rendered unconscious first to numb any pain. This is typically done with an intramuscular or intravenous injection of a sedative. Only after the animal is unconscious should an agent be given that causes respiratory or cardiac arrest. A veterinarian will typically use a very high dose of a barbiturate to painlessly remove the turtle from its suffering.

Hibernation and Breeding

T he long survival of box turtle species through the ages is due in part to their adaptation to natural climatic changes. They become inactive or dormant when weather conditions are cold, or excessively dry or hot. Hibernation (or brumation) is the turtle's response to cold conditions, while estivation serves them well during dry or hot times when food sources become scarce. Although box turtles instinctively know what to do, the pet owner must provide the proper conditions for safe hibernation. Emergence from hibernation signals another year of reproduction for adult turtles. Step-by-step instructions on the care of breeding-age turtles, egg incubation, and hatchling husbandry will give the pet owner the best chance for raising healthy new box turtles.

Hibernation in Nature

Box turtles that live in the cooler climates of North America will react to environmental cues that signal the onset of cold temperatures, harsh conditions, and lack of food. These cold-blooded animals warm their bodies directly from the sun or from objects that radiate the sun's warmth. Lower temperatures impair their ability to move limbs, digest food, and function normally. Cold temperatures, strong barometric lows, shorter daylight hours— even the lower angle of the sun—are all factors that can trigger the hibernation response in turtles. Wild turtles react to these conditions by overwintering in friable soil that allows them to dig below the freeze depth. Once dug in, they enter into a state of torpor. Your pet turtles will have the

Chapter 6 Glossary

carnula: Bony projection on the end of a hatching turtle's beak used to pierce its egg shell; often called an egg tooth

nest cavity: A flask-shaped hole for egg deposition that a female turtle digs with her hind limbs

Most box turtles hibernate in the wild, but a few tropical species such as the keeled box turtle do not.

same instincts, and you will have to accommodate them.

Although turtle keepers call this behavior brumation or hibernation, it is quite different from the behavior of the hibernating bear that sleeps in a cozy den and lives off large stores of fat. Box turtles do not store fat for winter. They take shelter under thick vegetation, tree roots, rodent burrows, or stump holes, or they dig into the sides of hills or muddy banks as the temperatures drop. If they are lucky, additional leaves may fall on them for added protection. As winter progresses, they will dig deeper into the ground. Ornate box turtles in Wisconsin have been found 3 feet (1 m) below ground! During hibernation the heart rate slows, breathing and metabolism are reduced, and energy consumption drops to a fraction of summertime usage. Winter is a dangerous time for box turtles, and some die each year as a result of inadequate freeze protection. Flooding and predators also kill many box turtles each winter and early spring. Knowing the pitfalls of hibernation will help you to overwinter your box turtles safely.

Hibernation vs. Brumation

Reptiles don't actually hibernate— they brumate. Hibernation is a process by which animals prepare for winter by eating large amounts of food to build up extra body-fat reserves. The stored fat provides sustenance during the sleep periods. Box turtles and other reptiles have a small amount of fat reserves and survive only because they become dormant. Both processes involve the reduction of metabolism to conserve energy during winter, so the terms hibernation and brumation are often used interchangeably when discussing box turtles.

Box turtles from tropical or semi-tropical regions, where temperatures and food supplies remain relatively constant, do not hibernate. Neither the Malayan nor the keeled box turtles hibernate, but they may become dormant (estivate) during dry periods while awaiting the return of more favorable conditions. Hibernation and periods of dormancy are often linked to the hormonal cycles in breeding-age turtles. These cycles may impact the fertility of females and regulate the production of sperm in males. For this reason, breeders will want to learn when and for how long their species of turtle hibernates so they can provide conditions that better match the seasonal breeding cycles.

As the winter season approaches, some indoor-housed turtles will refuse to eat. They may be responding to the subtle environmental changes by attempting to begin hibernation. In this situation (refusal to eat), it is dangerous to keep the turtle awake at normal temperatures. Illness, even death, can occur. In this chapter I will discuss safe ways to hibernate your box turtles outside, describe several methods for artificial hibernation, and provide ways to encourage them to stay active all winter long. My turtles have successfully hibernated for many years. It affords me some time off from turtle care and more time to pursue other interests.

Should Your Turtle Hibernate?

Hibernation is natural for many species of box turtles but not an absolute necessity. For inexperienced keepers, or in the case of newly acquired or sick turtles, it may be best to keep them active during the winter. Turtles with internal worms or respiratory infections will only get worse during hibernation. By providing summer-like conditions, you can break the urge for hibernation and keep the turtle eating throughout the winter.

Do not hibernate a turtle showing any of the following signs. Take it to a veterinarian for proper assessment and treatment:

- Any aural swelling or lump on the head
- Any open wound that has not healed and is vulnerable to infection
- Dry, flaky skin—indicative of dehydration or vitamin deficiencies
- Mucous discharge from the eyes, nose, or mouth
- Runny or dry, shriveled stools, which could indicate parasites or dehydration
- Swollen or closed eyes
- Underweight, or light, hollow feel when held in hand
- Very pale or whitish tongue

Hibernation should only be allowed for healthy turtles that have eaten well all summer. Sick turtles will not have the reserve of energy required to survive the long winter. A pre-hibernation check-up from the veterinarian is a good idea for keepers inexperienced in the signs of turtle illnesses. Make sure to test for internal worms.

Hatchlings and very young or newly acquired turtles should not be hibernated. Keep them awake and indoors during the winter. Maintain moist bedding at all times and increase the temperature a few degrees. Have the lights stay on 14 hours a day and use a new UVB bulb to ensure vitamin D3 synthesis. These small changes will usually break the turtle's urge to hibernate. Turtles are more likely to retain their appetites if given plenty of live insects and whole prey foods. These are available for purchase year-round. Pieces of steamed fish and box turtle pellet food can also be used along with fruits, vegetables, and greens.

Florida box turtles go dormant for a shorter period of time than the typical box turtle hibernation period.

Dormant Periods

Some species like the Florida box turtle and certain Asian varieties (keeled and flowerback) do not typically hibernate, but they may benefit from a period of dormancy. You can provide this by following the normal hibernating procedures and shortening the duration time. Some hobbyists have successfully hibernated yellow-margined box turtles outdoors, but this should only be attempted after years of experience and careful planning.

Preparing the Turtle for Hibernation

After you have received a clean bill of health from the veterinarian, you can begin preparations for the hibernation process. Start offering more vegetable matter rich in vitamin A during the last month of warm weather. These include sweet potatoes, carrots, pumpkin, mangoes, and winter squashes. If your turtle is not consuming enough vitamin A-

Preparations for Hibernating Indoor Turtles

Indoor turtles should not be fed for two weeks prior to lowering temperatures. Soak daily in tepid water to hydrate and clear the intestine of wastes. After maintaining optimum temperatures for two weeks, gradually lower the heat in 5° F (3° C) increments over the course of several more weeks. Once the turtle becomes sluggish, place it into its hibernation site (hibernaculum).

rich foods, use cod liver oil as a supplement. It can be purchased in gel caps made for human consumption. Open the capsules and add a drop of cod liver oil on a favorite food item several times during this period. If the treated foods are refused, try injecting a drop into a wax worm or small earthworm, or even directly into the mouth. Do not give your turtles more than a couple of drops of this supplement over the entire month. Vitamin A is fat soluble and is stored in the body for use throughout the winter.

Turtles housed outdoors will begin to eat less and become inactive as cooler temperatures approach. At this point you should stop feeding the turtle, but continue to provide clean soaking water every day. The daily soakings will facilitate the vitally important process of clearing the turtle's gut. Before hibernating my outdoor turtles, I bring each one inside for a final soaking in tepid water. This is a good time to check stools for pinworms or discolored urine. I also record their weight and conduct a thorough examination, looking for cuts or lumps on the skin, nasal discharge, or signs of mouth rot.

The Hibernation Site

Prepare the hibernation site before autumn to avoid being caught off guard with a sleepy turtle that refuses to eat. Choosing the best site requires research and planning. Box turtles can hibernate in the ground, in a modified refrigerator, or in a box placed in a shed, crawl space, attic, or garage.

Refrigerators are a good choice when hibernating turtles in warm climates. The primary consideration is the capability to safely maintain a temperature range of 45° to 50° F (7° to 10° C) and humidity between 75 and 80 percent. I strongly urge owners to monitor the prospective site for an entire winter before actually placing turtles in their hibernacula. Areas prone to deep ground freeze and those exposed to wind or spring flooding are not good locations. If planning to use an artificial box or refrigerator, be sure that stable temperatures can be reliably maintained all winter long.

Outdoor Hibernation

Owners who live within the natural range of their box turtles can allow healthy turtles to hibernate in the ground. Each hibernaculum should be located within the pen and protected from predators. Make sure the site will be above the water table during spring.

In late summer or early fall, use a shovel to loosen up an area at least 3 feet (1 m) square by 2 to 3 feet (0.6 to 1 m) deep, depending on the maximum freeze depth in your region. Remove some of the dirt and then mix in composted leaves, peat moss, and grass clippings. Finally, run water into the pit to create a moist substrate into which the turtles can easily dig downward. After the turtles enter the pit, add enough mulched leaves, straw, and grass clippings until you have several feet of overlying mulch. If your region gets lots of rainfall, create an overhead shelter using plywood and cement blocks.

Although many keepers use this outdoor method to simulate natural hibernacula, there are inherent risks. It is not easy to check on the turtles' health, and it can be difficult to know if they have dug in deep enough. Mice, rats, and other predators can harm or kill hibernating turtles. Just like their wild counterparts, pet turtles overwintering outdoors are subject to the perils of hibernation.

Hibernation Box

My box turtles live outdoors during the spring, summer, and fall but are overwintered in a hibernation box located in an outbuilding. This allows me to check on the turtles and protect them from predators. Because the outbuilding has electrical service, I am able to

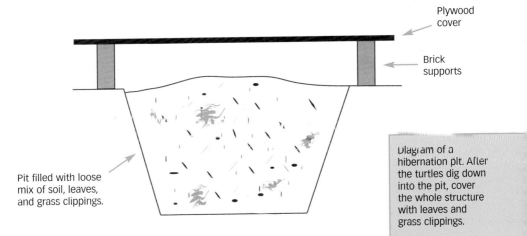

Plywood cover

Brick supports

Pit filled with loose mix of soil, leaves, and grass clippings.

Diagram of a hibernation pit. After the turtles dig down into the pit, cover the whole structure with leaves and grass clippings.

Tess Cook's Hibernation Box

These are plans for building the hibernation box used by the author. The final size of the box is 41 1/2 in. wide x 31 1/2 in. deep x 25 in. high, or 105.4 cm x 80.0 cm x 64.1 cm

Materials List

One and a half sheets of 4 ft x 8 ft x 3/4 in. plywood; (122 cm x 244 cm x 1.9 cm)

Three sturdy hinges

Two wooden knobs

Deck or drywall screws

Several feet (1-2 m) of 14-2 Romex wire

Electrical supply cord that will connect to a 120V outlet

Two ceramic light fixtures

Two 25-watt incandescent bulbs

One 120V thermostat used for baseboard heaters (not the low voltage type for furnaces)

One single-width junction box

One accurate digital thermometer with wireless remote display

One 4 ft. x 4 ft. (122 cm x 122 cm) sheet of 2 in. (5.1 cm) rigid insulation board

Lumber Dimensions

Cut lumber for the top half:

- Two short-side pieces 7 3/4 in. x 30 in. (19.7 cm x 76.2 cm)
- Two long-side pieces 7 3/4 in. x 41 1/2 in. (19.7 cm x 105.4 cm)
- Top piece 31 1/2 in. x 41 1/2 in. (80.0 cm x 105.4 cm); the top piece is attached to the upper edges of the side pieces.
- One board 6 in. x 15 in. (15.2 cm x 38 cm) to be used as baffle.

Cut lumber for the bottom half:

- Two short-side pieces 16 in. x 30 in. (40.6 cm x 76.2 cm)
- Two long-side pieces 16 in. x 41 1/2 in. (40.6 cm x 105.4 cm)
- Bottom piece 31 1/2 in. x 41 1/2 in. (80.0 cm x 105.4 cm); the bottom piece attaches to the lower edges of the sides.

Construction Steps

1. The top and bottom portions of the box are built separately and are assembled using drywall screws. Pre-drill the screw holes to avoid splitting the plywood. Build the top and bottom using the same arrangement of side pieces to avoid a mismatch when hinged together.
2. Join the completed top and bottom sections along the long side using the three hinges.
3. Affix the two ceramic light fixtures and junction box to the inside of the top unit. Space the lights about 15 to 18 inches (38 to 45.7 cm) apart for more even heating. Position the junction box as far from the lights as possible. Attach the baffle so that it shields the thermostat from direct heating by the lights.
4. Connect the lights in parallel and run the Romex wire to the junction box.
5. Mount the thermostat on the junction box and make the electrical connections to the electric supply cord (white to white; ground to ground; black wires connect to the thermostat terminals). Put the cord through a hole in the back side of the top. If not experienced with electrical wiring, get a licensed electrician to assist you.
6. Put the knobs on the front and drill three 1/4 in. (0.64 cm) diameter holes on each side of the top for ventilation.
7. The rigid insulation board (optional) is placed beneath the completed box to help insulate the unit from a cold floor or to keep bugs out when the unit is on a dirt floor.

Place the box in a cold area (with electric service) such as an outbuilding, detached garage, root cellar, or crawlspace. Monitor the temperatures and adjust the thermostat to maintain a temperature of 45° to 50° F (7° to 10° C) in the box. Do not put your turtles in until sure that the temperature is being maintained at the correct level. The outbuilding I use has baseboard heaters, and I set the building temperature to about 40° F (4.4° C). This results in less frequent use of the internal "heat" lights and helps reduce moisture loss within the box.

Hibernation Conditions

Proper temperature for artificially hibernated box turtles is 45° to 50° F (7° to 10° C). Relative humidity should be maintained between 75 and 80 percent.

maintain proper hibernation temperatures without worrying about freezing. Other keepers have used modified greenhouses and add supplemental heat only during the coldest part of winter.

A materials list and directions for building a hibernation box are provided in an accompanying sidebar. The construction of the box is easy, but it is heavy! Build the box close to where it will be placed. If you want a smaller box, just reduce the materials list and halve the width and length. The height of the box should remain the same in order to keep the light bulbs at a safe distance above the turtles.

Once the hibernation box is complete, you will have to place your turtles in containers within it; you don't just put them in there loose. Drill a dozen 1/4 inch. (0.64 cm) diameter holes in the lid of a plastic shoe or sweater box. Fill half the box with rinsed sphagnum moss. Squeeze most of the water out of the moss, but keep it moist. Place one turtle in each plastic box, close the top, and place it inside the hibernation box. Check on your turtle often to be sure the temperature and humidity are being maintained. I use a wireless digital thermometer/hygrometer with a remote receiver to check the box conditions daily.

If your turtles have been housed outside, they can be placed into the hibernation box soon after they have shown signs of slowing down. If normally kept inside, begin their cool-down about two weeks prior to placing into the hibernation box. Follow the process described earlier to prepare them for hibernation.

Refrigerator Hibernation

Box turtles housed indoors should not overwinter in the ground. When continually kept in warm climates they may lose the urge to hibernate and will continue to eat throughout the winter. Some turtles, however, may become sluggish and refuse to eat when late fall arrives. It is dangerous to allow turtles to "hibernate" in indoor setups. Household temperatures are not cold enough. These turtles are starving to death, not hibernating! It must be cool enough for them to enter a state of torpor (low energy expenditure). Use of a modified dorm refrigerator is one of the better solutions to the indoor hibernation problem.

Female eastern box turtle digging into an outdoor hibernaculum.

Preparations for hibernating your turtle in a refrigerator are the same you would use for overwintering outside. Use a dedicated small dorm refrigerator for hibernation. Family-size refrigerators are okay to use if dedicated solely to hibernating turtles. Otherwise, they may be too cold and cause the turtle undue stress from constant door opening. Adjust the refrigerator temperature to the ideal range of 45° to 50° F (7° to 10° C) prior to placing the turtle inside. Use a digital thermometer for accurate monitoring—preferably one that will send readings to a remote display and signal an alarm for out-of-range temperatures. If you are often away from home, a device can be purchased that will send an alert to your cell phone.

Once temperatures are stable, place the turtle in a medium-size plastic container lined with moist sphagnum moss (about half full). The container should have about a dozen 1/4 inch. (0.64 cm) diameter holes drilled into the top to insure a regular exchange of oxygen. Once in place, opening the refrigerator door a few minutes each day will usually provide enough oxygen, unless the refrigerator is packed with turtles. Crowded conditions will require a constant exchange of oxygen. Do this by inserting a 1-inch (2.54 cm) diameter tube (approximately 10 in. (25 cm) long) through a hole drilled in the top portion of the door. Cold air inside the refrigerator will settle towards the bottom, so make sure to place the turtles and thermometer as low as possible.

On-Going Health Checkups

A box turtle should not lose more than 10 percent of its body weight during

The Five Pitfalls of Hibernation

1. Equipment breakdown.
2. Predators attack hibernating turtles.
3. Temperatures are too warm or too cold for safe hibernation.
4. The ground is too wet or too dry.
5. Turtle is sick or lightweight and dies during hibernation.

hibernation. Healthy turtles will lose only an ounce or two (28 to 57 gms). I take my turtles out every other week during the first month to soak them in tepid water. After that, I check on them monthly until early spring, at which time I go back to the two-week schedule. If you notice any signs of illness such as dehydration, weight loss, swollen eyes, runny nose, or restlessness, remove the turtle from hibernation. Do this by gradually warming it over the course of a week. Never allow a sick turtle to remain cold. Address any health problems immediately and seek veterinary care if warranted. Keep the turtle indoors in summer-like conditions until it has been symptom-free for several months.

Renewal

Box turtles will begin to emerge from their outdoor hibernacula when nighttime temperatures stay above the high 50s F (about 14° C) and daytime temperatures reach the 60s F (about 17° C). They will not typically begin eating until daytime temperatures are somewhat warmer. However, they should be provided fresh water on a daily basis. Check carefully for any signs of disease, damage, or weight loss. I bring each turtle indoors and soak it in tepid water while looking for signs of mouth or shell rot, eye infection, or discharges from the nares, mouth, or cloaca. It is not unusual for the turtle to have thick urates the first time it evacuates. Females may discharge a bit of yolky material with their urine. Keep a look out for internal worms in the stool and see a veterinarian if worms are present. Light-weight turtles should be immediately housed in the hospital tank. Start feeding as soon as their core temperature has warmed up.

North American box turtles hibernate outside for about five months, from late October to March. Turtles that have been artificially hibernated can be awakened when the weather is milder or whenever the owner wants to begin providing summer-like conditions indoors. Box turtles should never be hibernated longer than is normal for their species. The feeding season should last as long as possible to ensure good health. Refrigerator hibernation for North American box turtles should only last about three months. You can extend this time if waiting for warmer outdoor conditions in the spring. If the turtles will be housed indoors,

Box turtles are ready to breed shortly after emerging from hibernation.

gradually raise the refrigerator temperature to near room temperature before moving them to their normal set-up. The dormancy period for non-hibernating species should last about six to eight weeks.

The mysterious behavior of hibernation in box turtles seems to be a time of renewal. Many believe it reduces stress, invigorates the turtles' immunity, and sets the timing of their hormonal cycles. One thing does seem apparent— box turtles are ready to reproduce after the long sleep!

Breeding Your Box Turtles

Box turtles take many years to become sexually mature. Although they hatch from the egg looking like a miniature of their parents, it takes between 8 and 12 years for turtles to reach breeding age. The survival of wild populations depends on their ability to successfully procreate. Turtle eggs and hatchlings are preyed upon by myriad predators including fire ants, skunks, raccoons, ravens, dogs—even rats and chipmunks! Many of these predators, especially raccoons and rats, are more common when humans arrive in the area and bring their gardens and garbage. Box turtle survival rate is low—only a few out of a hundred reach maturity in the wild. Because of this, it is vitally important that we never remove turtles from the wild.

Faced with the knowledge of declining populations, it might seem that captive-turtle breeding is a high priority for the turtle keeper. In certain cases it is. Most Asian box turtles are on the verge of extinction. These species may not currently have the government or local protection necessary to ensure survival in their natural home ranges. Thankfully, there are chelonian conservation organizations (see Resource section) working to preserve habitats and promote breeding of these endangered animals.

Captive box turtles do not need to procreate to have fulfilling lives, although males are well known for their determination in doing so! Some states require the males and females to be housed in separate pens, and allow breeding only by special permit. Whatever the case, it is important that breeding be a well-planned event—not an accidental occurrence. One needs to consider both the cost and the future care arrangements for the captive-bred turtles. There will be added veterinarian bills and extra live food to buy. If you will not be keeping all of the new turtles, have an adoption plan that includes people capable and willing to provide the proper care.

The Breeding Pair

Box turtles raised in captivity become sexually mature faster than their wild counterparts. They benefit from the regular and abundant food that helps them to grow and develop

Sex Characteristics of Several Species of Box Turtles

	T. carolina	*T. ornata*	*C. amboinensis*	*C. flavomarginata*
Eye color	M: red or pinkish F: brown	M: red F: brown	Sexes similar	Sexes similar
Head color	Sexes similar	M: green or yellow F: dark brown	Sexes similar	Sexes similar
Back claws	M: thick, curved F: slender, straight	M: first toe on hind limb moves inward	Sexes similar	Sexes similar
Tail	M: long, muscular with vent well past edge of plastron F: short with vent close to body	M: long, muscular with vent well past edge of plastron F: short with vent close to body	M: long, muscular with vent well past edge of plastron F: short with vent close to body	M: long, muscular with vent well past edge of plastron F: short with vent close to body
Plastron	M: concave F: flat (Three-toeds: sexes similar)	M: slightly concave F: flat	M: concave F: flat	M: concave F: flat
Shell size	M: sometimes larger	F: sometimes larger	Sexes similar	Sexes similar

In most species, female box turtles (top) have shorter tails than males with the vent positioned closer to the body. The male's tail (bottom) is longer and thicker and has the vent positioned further from the body, past the edge of the plastron.

faster. Determining whether you have both the male and female turtles needed for a breeding pair is not always straightforward. Sexing of young box turtles cannot normally be done until secondary external characteristics appear. Miniature laparoscopic equipment exists and allows researchers or veterinarians to distinguish males from females, but the use of such equipment is limited because of the high cost. Secondary sex characteristics begin to appear when the carapace length is about 3.5 inches (9 cm). Determining sex in box turtles can still be quite difficult. The key features useful in distinguishing sex are listed in an accompanying chart.

Courtship and Mating

Mating can occur anytime of the year for turtles kept indoors. Outdoor turtles usually mate during warm days in the spring and again in late summer. Box turtle courtship is not very elaborate. The male will peer at the female, eventually cornering her and pushing her with his head or forelegs while nipping at her shell. Aquatic box turtles swim above the female and claw at her head and shell.

When a male first approaches another turtle, he is unsure whether it is female. Holding his head high, he puffs out his neck to smell the air and flash the colorful scales located there. He will look closely at the other turtle's response. A female might pull her head and legs into her shell and close up. The male will respond to this defensive posture and begin his courtship. An immature or submissive male may exhibit behaviors similar to a female and end up getting mounted by the other male.

If two adult males encounter each other while on mating searches, a fight often breaks out! The males circle each other and lower the two legs facing the other turtle. This presents the other male with a vision of its shell while protecting the legs. Evenly matched turtles may bite at each other's heads and carapaces. The bites are so vicious that pieces of shell can be removed and injury can occur. One turtle will eventually back down and turn away to run for cover.

Females that have been approached by an interested male do not always close up in their shells. Sometimes they respond by biting and may actually get a very strong grasp on the male's limb. A receptive female may try to run away, but the male follows and will eventually be allowed to mount her. The male inserts his back feet into the inguinal pockets of the female (located in front of her back legs). She then closes the back portion of her shell firmly on his back legs. Male three-toeds will also use their forelimb claws to grab at carapace pits located on the pleural scutes of some females. A mating pair can remain coupled in this manner for hours. In many species, the male has a concave area on the plastron that facilitates mating.

Fertilization of the eggs occurs internally. The male wraps his long, muscular tail around the female's tail and positions their cloacas together. He then strains and leverages in order to evert his penis for sperm transfer to the female. The male will assume many precarious positions during mating, from upright on the edge of his shell to horizontally on his back with his legs in a terrible twist. Males are often quite weak after copulating and will typically hide until leg strength returns.

Wanderlust

Field research has shown that some young male box turtles are more transient than their female siblings and will move out of their mother's home range while seeking mates. Most females spend their whole lives in relative proximity to where they were hatched.

Housing Your Breeding Group

Turtles do not mate for life, and the two sexes should normally be housed separately. This is especially true for the more aggressive aquatic Malayan and three-striped turtles. Separate housing will allow females to eat in peace and

If you keep different species or subspecies of box turtles, house them separately to prevent accidental hybridization or intergradation. Here a male three-toed box turtle mates with a female Florida box turtle.

dig their nests without fear of disturbance by males. Mating needs to take place only once a year, or even less often. Females can store sperm in special folds within the oviducts for up to four years. This adaptation probably results from their solitary nature and the fact that contact with others in the wild is a chance occurrence.

If you must house females and males together, use a large enclosure with lots of vegetation and hiding places. The females can use these to escape the attention of the male. Males of the same species can rarely be housed together. I have had some luck keeping males of different subspecies together. It is likely that some of the visual cues used for attacking rival males are unique to each type.

Another important ingredient for successful breeding is the overall health of the turtles. Considerable energy is needed to mate, produce eggs, and dig nests. Breeding also increases stress on the turtles. Several years of proper nutrition and excellent care should be provided before attempting to breed your turtles. Always have cuttlebone in the female's pen and add calcium powder to food once each week. Turtles have died because of complications resulting from breeding, so every precaution should be taken to ensure their health and safety.

Nesting

In the wild, gravid (pregnant with eggs) females usually dig nests from May to July. The eggs are incubated by the sun and develop into hatchlings without parental care. In captive situations, females may be unable to find sites suitable for nest building and successful incubation. Before eggs are produced you need to plan for proper nest-building conditions. Keepers can leave the eggs in the ground if they live within the normal home range or climate of their particular box turtle. Many people use this method with success. Females can lay eggs about three weeks after mating. If conditions are ideal, multiple clutches are possible, with a separation of about three weeks between each one.

Several days prior to laying her eggs, a female box turtle may stop eating—even refusing her favorite foods. She will pace in the enclosure and may dig some test holes. Gravid turtles housed indoors must be provided a suitable area for nest digging. A large plastic tub—22 in. x 16 in. (55 cm x 41 cm)—with 6 to 8 inches (15 to 20 cm) of moist, sandy soil and an overhead heat lamp will usually entice the female to dig a nest and lay her eggs. Females living outside will often begin nest digging in the late afternoon. The female begins by picking a spot to her liking such as a sunny open area, next to a rock, or under a shrub. She firmly plants her front feet on the ground and, if grass is present, uses her back feet to pull the grass and other debris away from the surface. She then alternately uses both rear claws to remove dirt and dig a flask-shaped hole, 3.5 to 4 inches (8.9 to 10.2 cm) deep. Each foot-full of dirt is piled near the hole. The toes are used to scrape the walls of the hole and create a smooth surface. If a root or large rock is encountered, she will abandon the hole and start a new one later on, possibly the next day. Female turtles are very picky about their nests and will go to great lengths

Gravidity Test

You can check to see whether a female turtle is gravid by palpating her hindquarters. With the turtle facing away from you, gently pull her hind legs out of the shell so that you can place one or two fingers into the inguinal pockets (soft area immediately in front of each hind leg). Gently rock the female from side to side as you probe the soft body tissue for evidence of eggs.

Indoor box turtles will nest in plastic tubs that have a deep layer of moist sandy soil in the bottom.

to dig a deep hole. The entire process may take more than four hours, often finishing in darkness.

The Egg Stage When the female has finished digging her nest, the egg-laying process begins. She may pull her head in and hiss as the cloaca expands to pass the eggs. Once the eggs have been deposited, the female is able to carefully position each egg solely by the dexterity and sensitivity in her legs. Subsequent eggs are deposited at intervals of a few minutes. Egg size is quite variable even for a given species. They are thin-shelled (flexible), elliptical, and translucent-white with a pale pinkish glow when first laid. Malayan and Chinese three-striped eggs are brittle-shelled. Clutch size varies from one to seven eggs, depending on the species.

After all the eggs have been deposited, the female may first add some of the grass that was piled up near the hole. Then she'll push some dirt over the eggs. Next she puts her leg into the hole to repeatedly tamp the dirt. Another foot-full of dirt is added and then more tamping. In this manner she builds a hard cap over the eggs. When completely filled in, she will use her legs and plastron for a final tamping. She may even replace pebbles and twigs, effectively leaving no hint that a nest was ever constructed!

Even if you decide to artificially incubate the eggs, you should allow the turtle to dig her

A Simple Homemade Incubator

Making an incubator for your turtle eggs is fairly easy. You will need:

- **A 10-gallon (38 l) glass aquarium**
- **One to five small plastic containers (cottage cheese or margarine tubs, cleaned and disinfected)**
- **One or more incandescent lamps**
- **Digital thermometer**
- **Sphagnum moss or coarse vermiculite**

Fill the aquarium with very moist sphagnum moss. This bedding will create a humid environment within the tank. Poke several large holes into the sides of the plastic containers near the top to allow for excess water drainage. Fill the containers with moist sphagnum moss or moist vermiculite. Make a depression in the bedding; if it fills with water, it's too wet. Remove some water by blotting with paper towels.

Place the eggs in the depression. Put a digital thermometer near the eggs and mount the incandescent lamp about 10 inches (25 cm) above the eggs. Adjust the wattage and height of the lamp until you can maintain a temperature of 84° F (29° C) for the duration of the incubation. Cover any openings on top of the tank with aluminum foil to reduce evaporation. Do not let the nesting medium dry out. Add distilled water to the egg container's medium as needed to maintain moisture.

nest, lay and cover the eggs. This is a strong instinct in females, and they should be permitted to finish the job. If you decide to leave the eggs in the ground, fashion a chicken wire box and place it over the area and stake it down. Raccoons, skunks, even other female turtles can dig up the nest if it is left unprotected. The box will allow any hatchlings to surface, yet not escape. Depending on the nest temperatures, the eggs can hatch in 60 to 90 days. Late-developing turtles may even overwinter in the nest and emerge in the spring.

Egg Incubation

If planning to use an incubator, have one ready *before* the turtle lays her eggs. You can buy a commercial incubator or make your own. Commercial poultry and reptile incubators have been successfully used by many hobbyists to incubate lizard, snake, and turtle eggs.

Purchase an incubator with a built-in thermostat, preferably a pulse-proportional thermostat. This is a device that regulates temperature by increasing and decreasing the power as the temperature fluctuates. Buy a good thermometer that includes a humidity gauge. Be sure to adjust the temperature before placing the eggs inside. This may take several days, so start the process well before the eggs are due. Many incubators are preset to the higher temperatures needed for hatching poultry eggs.

Most breeders incubate their eggs on coarse vermiculite, which is available in garden stores. These are hatching eastern box turtles.

Egg Medium The best medium for incubating eggs is coarse vermiculite, although many breeders have success with long-fiber sphagnum moss. Both offer good moisture content and retention properties. Both products should be rinsed and drained in a colander. Place the moist medium in small plastic containers to a depth of at least 3.5 inches (8.9 cm). Add distilled water equal to half the volume of the medium. Poke two holes three-fourths of the way up the plastic container so excess water can drain before reaching the eggs. The eggs should be surrounded by moist medium but should never be sitting in water. Use your thumb to make a slight depression in the medium and place the egg in the hole. If the depression fills with water, you have too much. Place an additional container of water in the incubator to add humidity. Ambient humidity near 85-90 percent is adequate.

Do not turn over or jostle the eggs when moving them to the incubator. Place them in the same orientation as you found them in the nest. Mark the top of the egg with a soft lead pencil. The embryo grows in a particular orientation, so rotating the egg could have a disastrous effect. Do not cover the egg with medium—allow half of it to remain exposed. The eggshell often takes on a chalky white color with time. Some Asian species will have a distinct band of white around the egg. This phenomenon is called "banding;" it signals the egg is fertile and contains a growing embryo. Place a loose-fitting cover on top of the container to allow fresh air exchange while minimizing evaporation. Add distilled water on a regular basis as needed to keep the medium moist. Never pour water directly onto the eggs.

Time and Temperature

Recent studies (H. Kalb, unpublished data) have been conducted using Malayan box turtle eggs to see how temperature variations affect incubation time. An empirical relationship was established that showed a decrease in incubation duration with increase in temperature. Eggs hatched after about 100 days when the incubation temperature was close to 75° F (24° C), and about 60 days when it was near 86° F (30° C).

Incubation Temperature

Box turtles do not have sex chromosomes. Sex is determined by nest temperature rather than a particular combination of chromosomes from the parents. The process is referred to as temperature-dependent sex determination (TSD). In box turtles, sex is probably assigned during a singular pivotal period in the incubation process. This temperature-sensitive period likely varies for each species. Incubation temperatures as low as room temperature and as high as 88° F (31° C) have been used successfully for box turtles. The lower range produces mostly males, while higher temperatures produce mostly females. In general, a good temperature to strive for is 84° F (29° C). This should result in hatchlings of both sexes, with perhaps a few more females on average.

Egg Development You can check the viability of the eggs two weeks after artificial incubation begins by using a method called "candling." With clean hands, gently remove the egg from the incubator and, without jarring or rotating the egg, look at it using a strong backlight (flashlight) in a darkened room. Place the light behind the egg to illuminate the inside. For turtle embryos, you will see a network of blood vessels around the yolk mass and perhaps a dark mass at the top. Do not despair if nothing is visible. Carefully return the egg to the incubator and check again in a few weeks.

The incubating egg will undergo several changes. It will appear to swell up and may change color. Some may show areas of green, purple, or brown. This coloration results from the byproducts released as the embryo grows. Unfertilized eggs harden and shrivel and will look yellow. It is normal that some fertilized eggs will fail to produce embryos. Some lack sufficient nutrients for full development. They can get either too hot or too cold. Eggs are also susceptible to mold and can be eaten by insects or parasites.

The Hatchlings

Box turtle hatchlings are cute creatures with their large eyes, little legs, and tiny claws. If all goes well, the egg will "pip" in 60 to 90 days, possibly longer depending on the incubation technique and temperature. The neonates have a carnula, or egg tooth, on the tip of the beak; it is used to tear open the eggshell in a process called pipping. An arm or head may peek out as the turtle begins to exit the egg. It may seem to be in distress, but is more likely just gulping air and flexing its shell and will usually be completely out soon after. Some neonates can remain in the shell for several days. They may still have a large external yolk sac attached to the plastron. A ruptured yolk sac could lead to death—never help the turtle out of its egg! Once drawn into the body, the remaining yolk can sustain the hatchling for an additional two to four weeks.

Abnormal neonates are not uncommon. They can have abnormal shells, extra scutes or toes, or a single nare. Albinos, eyeless heads, and twins have all been reported. The conditioning of the female probably plays a part in the health of her hatchlings. Older females tend to produce larger young. The typical carapace length of neonates (straight line method) varies from 1.5 to 2 inches (3.8-5.1 cm).

Example of an indoor pen for box turtle hatchlings. Note the digital thermometer and the timer for the lights.

Hatchling Housing

Box turtle hatchlings have soft, thin shells and can desiccate quickly under the hot sun or heat lamp. Their shell offers little protection, so they tend to hide most of the time and hunt close to cover (hatchlings are rarely seen in the wild). If they have been hatched outside, bring the hatchlings indoors so you can more easily keep them moist and warm and monitor their development. After several years (at about 3 inches (7.6 cm) long), they can be placed in an outdoor enclosure permanently.

Preventing injury and illnesses in young turtles is the best medicine. Many health problems result from poor husbandry. Keep their housing clean and provide adequate moisture, heat, and light. Dehydration, poor nutrition, parasites, and even carelessness have all been causes of premature death in hatchlings. Watch out for hatchlings that get stuck upside down or between furnishings, where they might overheat in the full glare of heat lamps. Young turtles can drown in oversized bowls if kept with adults, or may be attacked by ants or chipmunks if left outside.

Owners can use one of two types of housing to successfully raise box turtle hatchlings, the moist tank or the wet nursery tank. Either setup is suitable for hatchlings, and it is the owner's preference as to which one is used.

Moist Nursery The moist nursery setup uses a 10-gallon (38-liter) aquarium and is suitable for three to four hatchlings. Use a second aquarium if more hatchlings will be housed. The smaller tanks are easier to keep warm and moist. Cover the bottom with 2 inches (5.1 cm) of rinsed, moist cypress bark or coco-peat. Place moist sphagnum moss 3 to 4 inches deep (7.6 to 10.2 cm) on one side of the tank. Put a shallow saucer of water on the opposite side and recess it level to the substrate. A small hide can be placed on the moss. If hatchlings do not come to the water on their own, place them in the saucer on a daily basis. Mist the moss and bark frequently. Use a heat lamp to warm the moss area to about 75° F (24° C) and provide full-spectrum light (UVA and UVB). The cool end should not go below 70° F (21° C).

Save That Egg! You may be able to save a moldy egg by wiping off the mold with a wet paper towel. Handle the egg gently and do not rotate it. Return the egg to the incubator in an egg container with new moist substrate.

Wet Nursery The wet nursery tank has 1.5 inches (3.8 cm) of standing water at the low

Number of Eggs per Clutch for Several Species

Egg size and number of clutches vary by species and may even vary from one female to another within same species. Typically, more eggs are produced by large, healthy females. *Terrapene* eggs are about 1 to 1.7 inches (2.5 to 4.2 cm) measured on the long axis. *Cuora* eggs are slightly larger at 1.6 to 2 inches (4 to 5 cm).

Species	Number of eggs/clutch	Number of clutches/year
T. carolina	1 to 7	1 to 4
T. ornata	1 to 5	1 to 2
C. amboinensis	1 to 3	1 to 4
C. flavomarginata	1 to 3	1 to 3

end and is used to ensure the hatchlings never dry out (drying can deform the shell). Raise one side of the tank by placing a 2-inch-thick (5 cm) dowel or board under one end. Use only wet sphagnum moss to create a thick substrate on the high side of the tank. The water needs to be changed every few days, depending on the number of turtles. Feed the turtles in a separate container to extend the cleanliness of the water and substrate. Aggressive hatchlings may try to bite other turtles during feeding and should be fed separately.

Semi-aquatic Malayan and aquatic Chinese three-striped hatchlings should be housed in a wet nursery tank. However, the water depth should be increased to about 2 inches (5 cm). There should be a flat rock on the moss for the hatchlings to use when basking. The overhead light should not get too hot. Maintain a basking temperature of 82° F (28° C). As the hatchlings grow larger, remove the dowel and gradually increase the water depth and size of aquarium until they are ready for adult-size aquariums (about 3 years old).

Outdoor Hatchling Pen Wild turtle hatchlings do not have the benefit of someone watching over them. Many are killed and eaten. Others can starve, become dehydrated, or perish during the winter. But the outdoors is the box turtle's real home, and the benefits from sun and exercise cannot be overstated. A little time outside in the summer months is good for the hatchlings and can be safely provided with an outdoor hatchling pen. Make a wooden frame and attach chicken wire to the sides, top, and bottom—be sure to add a door! Place the pen directly on the ground in a sunny area. Use a wide board rather than cloth to create a partial

A gallery of box turtle hatchlings. Clockwise from top left: ornate, Mexican, Chinese three-striped, and yellow-margined.

sun screen. The pen should never be left unattended. Do not use glass tanks or dark-colored containers for temporary outdoor pens, as they can rapidly overheat.

Hatchling Diets

Hatchlings will not be hungry until their yolk has been used up. After a few weeks, entice them to eat by providing chopped-up earthworms or live insects such as small crickets, wax worms, freshly molted mealworms, or bloodworms. Isopods (pill bugs) are land-dwelling crustaceans that hatchlings readily accept. Asian hatchlings can be fed all of the above as well as pieces of steamed fish and pellet food made for aquatic turtles. Avoid using wild snails and slugs, as they can be an intermediate host for internal parasites.

When the young turtles begin to exhibit a hearty appetite, add tiny pieces of steamed winter squash, sweet potatoes, and other vegetables, fruits, and assorted greens to the diet. These foods may not appeal to them at first, but the new sights and smells will help them to be less finicky eaters later on. It is important to have these healthy foods available to the turtles when they are ready to eat them. My turtles (three-toeds and ornates) begin to eat plant material within four to six months after hatching.

The food should be chopped to a size suitable for the small turtle. A one-month-old hatchling might not be able to eat a whole grape or a large Canadian nightcrawler. A small turtle biting into the tough skin of a nightcrawler can get wrapped up like a capybara being crushed by an anaconda. Superworms and crickets can bite and should have their mouth parts pinched off before feeding to hatchlings. If young turtles will not eat vegetables, try dipping crickets and earthworms into jarred baby food. Use flavors such as carrots, sweet potatoes, and green beans.

Hatchling Heath Alert!

Is your hatchling's carapace beginning to curl up around the edges? Do you see a thickening around the edges of the shell? Do you see raised carapace scutes? These are common irregularities in baby turtle shells that result from improper humidity and excess protein in the diet. It is important to review your housing condition and diet in order to avoid these and other shell deformities.

Repatriation

Many keepers hope that one day they will be able to repatriate (release) their box turtles into suitable habitat. Asian box turtles may be dependent on captive breeding for their future viability. If involved with breeding, keepers should maintain detailed records and a stud book. However, the majority of turtle owners will not likely be called upon to provide turtles for conservation efforts. But we can help in other ways. Local education and conservation efforts need our support. Take the case of George Patton and Martha Ann Messinger. During the 1990s they spearheaded efforts to end the collection of Louisiana's box turtles for the pet trade. Based on these efforts, the Louisiana state legislature passed a law that provided for the protection of the state's native box turtles. It was a true testament to the power of the individual in making a difference!

Conservation Groups

The Tortoise Trust
BM Tortoise
London
WC1N 3XX
UK
http://www.tortoisetrust.org/

Turtle Conservation Fund
www.turtleconservation.org/

Turtle Survival Alliance
1989 Colonial Parkway
Fort Worth, Texas 76110
www.turtlesurvival.org/

World Chelonian Trust
P.O. Box 1445
Vacaville, CA 95696
www.chelonia.org/

Clubs and Societies

British Chelonia Group
P.O.Box 1176
Chippenham Wilts
SN15 1XB
UK
www.britishcheloniagroup.org.uk/

California Turtle & Tortoise Club
P.O. Box 7300
Van Nuys, CA 91409-7300
www.tortoise.org

The Chicago Turtle Clu
6125 N. Fairfield Ave.
Chicago, IL 60659
E-mail: chicagoturtle@geocities.com
www.geocities.com/Heartland/Village/7666/

German Chelonia Group
Im Bongert 11a
D-52428 Jülich
www.dght.de/ag/schildkroeten/english/
eschildkroeten.htm

Mid-Atlantic Turtle & Tortoise Society
P.O. Box 22321
Baltimore, MD 21203-4321
E-mail: matts@matts-turtles.org
www.matts-turtles.org/

New York Turtle and Tortoise Society
NYTTS
P.O. Box 878
Orange, NJ 07051-0878
E-mail: QandA@nytts.org
nytts.org/

Rescue and Adoption Services

PetFinder.com
www.petfinder.com

The Turtle Center
www.turtlecenter.org/

Turtle Homes
www.turtlehomes.org/

Veterinary Resources

Association of Reptile and Amphibian Veterinarians (ARAV)
P.O. Box 605
Chester Heights, PA 19017
Phone: 610-358-9530
Fax: 610-892-4813
E-mail: ARAVETS@aol.com
www.arav.org

Websites

Box Turtle Care and Conservation Webpage
(author's site)
www.boxturtlesite.info

Kingsnake.com
www.kingsnake.com

The Turtle Puddle (turtle care sheets)
www.turtlepuddle.org

Yahoo email groups
www.groups.yahoo.com

Alderton, D. 1988. *Turtles & Tortoises of the World*. Facts on File, Inc. 191 pp.

Barnett, S. L. and B. R. Whitaker. 2004. Indoor care of North American box turtles. *Exotic DVM Veterinary Magazine*. 6.1: 23-29.

Buskirk, J. May 1993. Yucatan box turtle, *Terrapene carolina yucatana*. *Tortuga Gazette*. 29 (5): 10-12.

———. 2002. The mysterious Mexican spotted box turtle, *Terrapene nelsoni* Stejneger, 1925. *RADIATA, Journal of German Chelonia Group*. 11 (1): 3-11.

Connor, M. J. and V. Wheeler. 1998. The Chinese box turtle, *Cistoclemmys flavomarginata* Gray 1863. *Tortuga Gazette*. 34 (10): 1-7.

Dodd, C. K. 2001. *North American Box Turtles: A Natural History*. University of Oklahoma Press. 231 pp.

Donoghue, S. and S. McKeown. 1999. Nutrition of captive reptiles. *Veterinary Clinics: Exotic Animal Practice*. 2.1: 69-91.

Ernst, C.H. and R.W. Barbour. 1989. *Turtles of the World*. Smithsonian Institution Press, Washington D.C. 313 pp.

Pfau, B. and J. Buskirk. 2006, Overview of the genus *Terrapene*, Merrem, 1820. *RADIATA, Journal of German Chelonia Group*. 15 (4): 3-31.

Highfield, A. C. 1996. *Practical Encyclopedia of Keeping and Breeding Tortoises and Freshwater Turtles*. Carapace Press, London, England. 295 pp.

Innis, C. 2001. Medical issues affecting the rehabilitation of Asian chelonians. *Turtle and Tortoise Newsletter*. 4: 14-16.

Klerks, M. 2005. Irrungen und Wirrungen bei der Identifizierung der Wisten-DosenschildkrŒte Terrapene ornata luteola Smith & Ramsey, 1952. *SchildkrŒten in Fokus*, Bergheim. 2 (1): 3-12.

Klingenberg, R. J. 1993. *Understanding Reptile Parasites, the Herpetocultural Library Special Edition*. Advanced Vivarium Systems Publishers, Lakeside, Ca. 81 pp.

Legler, J. M. 1960. Natural history of the ornate box turtle, *Terrapene ornata ornata* Agassiz. *University of Kansas Publications, Museum of Natural History*. 11 (10): 527-669.

Lindgren, J. 2004. UV-lamps for terrariums: Their spectral characteristics and efficiency in promoting vitamin D3 synthesis by UVB irradiation. *Herpetomania*. 13(3-4): 13-20.

McArthur, S. 1996. *Veterinary Management of Tortoises and Turtles*. Blackwell Science Ltd, Oxford. 170 pp.

Messinger, M. A. and G. M. Patton. 1995. Five year study of nesting of captive *Terrapene carolina triunguis*. *Herpetological Review*. 26 (4): 193-195

Minx, P. 1996. Phylogenetic relationships among the box turtles, genus *Terrapene*. *Herpetologica*. 52 (4): 584-597.

Schwartz, E. R., C. W. Schwartz, and A. R. Kiester. 1984. The three-toed box turtle in Central Missouri, part II: a nineteen-year study of home range, movements and population. *Missouri Department of Conservation, Terrestrial Series*, No. 12. 30 pp.

Senneke, D. and C. Tabaka, DVM. 2004. The Malayan box turtle (*Cuora amboinensis*). *World Chelonian Trust Website*.

Wiesner, C. S. and C. Iben. 2003. Influence of environmental humidity and dietary protein on pyramidal growth of carapaces in African spurred tortoises (*Geochelone sulcata*). *Journal of Animal Physiology and Animal Nutrition*. 87 (1-2): 66-74.

Wyneken, J. and D. Witherington. Chelonian anatomy poster. Zoological Education Network.

Note: **Boldfaced** numbers indicate illustrations; an italic *t* indicates tables.

plastron, **10**
  healthy, 31
  hinge of, **7**, 22–23
  sex differences in, 110t
pneumonia, 81
predators
  attacks by, 92–93, 109
  protection from, 43–44, 103
preferred optimal temperature zone, 38
probiotics, 91
prolapsed organs, 91–92
protozoans, parasitic, 86, 87–88

quarantine terrarium and care, 32–33, **33**
quick of nail, 76–77

refrigerator, hibernation in, 102, 106–107, 108–109
repatriation, 81, 123
rescue services, 30, 124
research on box turtles, 9
resources, 124
respiration, 23
respiratory infection, 72, 81–82
resuscitation of "dead" turtle, 79
runny nose syndrome, 81–82

Salmonella, 32, 38, 94–95, **95**
scales, 22
scientific names, 12
scutes, **10**, 18, 22
senses, 24
septicemia, 93
septicemic cutaneous ulcerative disease, 72, 82–84,
  84
sex characteristics, 23, 110t, 111, **111**
sex determination, temperature-dependent, 118
sexual maturity, 109, 110–111
shell, **10**, 22–23
  growth rings on, 18, 24
  healthy, 30–31
  irregular growth of, 74–76, **75**, 123
  sex differences in, 110t
shell fractures, **93**, 93–94
shell rot, 72, 82–84, **84**
sick turtles. *See* health problems
sight, sense of, 24
skeleton, **23**
smell, sense of, 24
soaking
  pre-hibernation, 100, 102
  of sick turtles, 71, 80, 81
societies and clubs, 30, 69, 124
Southeast Asian box turtle. *See* Malayan box turtle
species
  Asian, 16–21, **22**
  egg and clutch variations in, 121t
  habitat preferences of, 47
  housing considerations for, 33, 36–37, 39, **113**
  names of, 12
  North American, 10–16, **17**, **19**
  sex characteristics of, 110t
sphagnum moss, 47, 116, 117
spinach, 56, 59

spotted box turtles, 11, 14–15, **17**, 36
starvation, 86
sterile gut syndrome, 91
stomatitis, necrotic, 88–89
stress, 67
subspecies names, 12
substrate
  for egg incubation, 116, 117, **117**
  gut impaction by, 80, **80**
  for hospital tank, 70, 71
  indoor, 47–48, **49**
  maintenance of, 44, 51
  for nesting, 41
  outdoor, 40–41, 42, **43**
  types to avoid, 48, 77–78
supplements, 63–64, 79
  adding to meal, 60
  calcium, 59
  pre-hibernation, 101–102
swimming ability, 25

tail, 31, 110t, **111**
temperature
  body, 25, 36, 37
  egg incubation, 116, 117, 118
  feeding problems and, 77, 78
  hibernation, 102, 105, 106, 107, 108–109
  hospital tank, 71
  indoor habitat, 49
  outdoor pen, 39
  preferred optimal, 38
  quarantine, 33
temperature-dependent sex determination, 118
Terrapene species, 6, 10–16, **17**, **19**. *See also* North American
    box turtles
terrarium, quarantine, 32–33
terrestrial box turtles
  indoor habitat for, 46, 47
  quarantine terrarium for, 32–33
  species of, 47
Testudinidae family, 6
thermoregulation, 25, 36, 37
three-toed box turtle, 7, 11, 12–13, **13**
  drinking by, **90**
  feeding by, **54**
  mating by, **113**
  in outdoor pen, **40**
  shell deformity in, **75**
ticks, 73
toes, 24–25
tortoises, 5, 6, 10
trimming beak and nails, 76–77, **78**
turtle chow, 59
turtles
  history of, 5, 6, 10
  repatriation of, 81, 123
  tortoises vs., 6
tympanic scale, **10**, 24

ultraviolet light, 49–50, 75
upper respiratory tract disease, 72, 81–82

vegetables, 56–57, 58–59, 60, 61t
vent, 23, 110t, **111**
vermiculite, 116, 117, **117**
veterinarians, 68–69
  checkups by, 32, 68, **68**, 101
  euthanasia by, 95
  finding, 69
  illnesses requiring, 72
    when to see, 69
veterinary resources, 124
Vietnamese box turtle. *See* keeled box turtle
viral infections, 82
vitamin A
  deficiency of, 64, 85, 86, **87**
  supplemental, 101–102
  toxicity of, 85, **87**
vitamin D3, 64
  deficiency of, 75, 86
  ultraviolet light and, 50
vitamin deficiencies, 79, 86
vitamin supplements, 60, 64

water, need for, 64, 89–90, **90**
watering stations
  indoor, 48, 51
  outdoor, 42, 44, 45, **46**
weight, 30, 107–108
western box turtle. *See* ornate box turtles
wet nursery, 120–121
wild box turtles
  collection of, 28–29, 68
  diet of, 56, 61, 62
  hibernation by, **98**, 98–99
  injured, finding care for, 30
  protection of, 29, 109, 123
  range and habitat of, 36–37
  threats to, 6–7, 109
World Chelonian Trust, 69
worms
  for feeding, 57
  parasitic, 79, 86–87, 88
wounds, superficial, 71–72

yellow-margined box turtle, 17, 19–20, **21**
  diet for, 56, 61, 62
  dormant period for, 101
  eggs of, 121t
  examining, **71**
  habitat of, 37
  handling, **95**
  hatchling of, **122**
  housing for, 49, 52
  parasites in, **89**
  sex characteristics of, 110t
yolk sac, 119
Yucatan box turtle, 11, 14, **15**, 36

zoonoses, 94–95

Photo Credits:

6958509845 (courtesy of Shutterstock): 32; Randall D. Babb: 19 (center); Joan Balzarini: 34, 43, 68; Colin & Sandy Barnett: 11, 46, 56, 65; R. D. Bartlett: 16, 17 (bottom), 89, 101, 122 (top left, top right, bottom right); Suzanne L. Collins: 8, 13, 96, and back cover; Tess Cook: 7, 40, 41, 90, 105, 111; David Davis (courtesy of Shutterstock): 3, 10 Jimmy Dunlap: 75; Raymond Farrell: 122 (bottom left); Paul Freed: 98; James E. Gerholdt: 54; Michael Gilroy: 21, 95; George Grall: 50; Dr. Joseph E. Heinen: 115; Mary Hopson: 52; Dr. Heather Kalb: 119; Wayne Labenda: 107, 109; Jerry R. Loll: 113; Peter J. Mayne: 17 (top); Sean McKeown: 15 (bottom), 71; Stephanie Moore: 103; Paula Morris (from Wyneken, J. and D. Witherington): 23; Ian Murray: 19 (bottom), 58; Kenneth T. Nemuras: 1, 21 (top); Aaron Norman: 20, 80; Mella Panzella: 62, 66, and cover; M.P. & C. Piednoir: 22 (top); Dr. Peter Pritchard: 73; Annabel Ross: 74; Mark Smith: 26; Michael Smoker: 22 (bottom); Tim Spuckler: 45; Karl H. Switak: 4, 14, 15 (top), 19 (top), 28, 33, 36, 87; Dr. Chris Tabaka: 49, 76, 78, 85, 92, 93; Brian Wallace: 84; All others from T.F.H. Archives